AMATEUR DRAMATICS CAN BE MURDER

A Saffron Weald Mystery

Ann Sutton

Wild Poppy Publishing

To my little Zelie Sabine

Amateur Dramatics Can Be Murder
By
Ann Sutton
Book 4
Saffron Weald Mysteries

Prologue

The ancient, iron-studded prison door, silent witness to thousands of convicts passing over its threshold, today faced just one: a hulking, mountainous figure who filled the narrow corridor with menace. A small, rusted grating let in the sweet air of freedom moments before the warden unlocked the door. He had served his time. The scales of justice were now in balance. Time to retrieve the prize.

The clank of keys and crunch of iron turning in the lock sounded like birdsong to his ears.

The warden pushed open the timeworn door which squealed on hinges gasping for oil.

"And don't come back!" wheezed the jailor through stained teeth, his listless eyes red behind greasy hair, as he shoved the ex-convict roughly and slammed the door.

The freed prisoner stood, breathing in the gritty, urban air, bemused while people scurried past, barely glancing his way.

He fingered the few coins in his pocket.

Where to now?

CHAPTER 1

Scripts, squabbles and storms.

Tension crackled like a bolt of lightning as biting cold February rain lashed the windows of the Saffron Weald village hall. Ophelia Harrington eyed the plate of almond cakes and cream buns Alice Puddingfield, the baker, had placed in the center of the table with the greed of a stray cat. Her fingers began the walk across the table.

"As chairman of the theatrical society, I believe *I* should have the final say," asserted Matilda Butterworth, owner of the teashop, raising her voice above the noise of the rain, her usually gentle demeanor hardening into something steelier. As Ophelia hastily withdrew her hand, she noticed Matilda's white knuckles clamped around the stack of papers before her.

Matilda's firm statement was instantly greeted with an angry hubbub of disagreement, headed by Mildred Chumbley, the busiest busybody Ophelia had ever had the displeasure to meet.

Matilda raised her hands as if to put a shield between herself and the impassioned group. "If everyone feels so heated about the situation, then perhaps we should put it to a secret ballot."

The comment brought the ugly rebellion to a sudden close.

As the rain drummed harder against the windows, and a draft whistled through the ill-fitting window frames, making the ancient curtains dance, Imogen Pettigrew reflected on the fact that the village hall had not changed at all since she and her twin sister, Ophelia, had performed here as schoolgirls over fifty years ago. Even the musty smell of damp wood and forgotten costumes remained the same.

"That seems like a more democratic idea," commented Patricia Snodgrass, the efficient postmistress, who sat in the chair next to Matilda. She ripped a piece of paper from her notepad, folded it into squares, tearing it carefully into equal pieces which she handed around the table.

Mildred cupped her hand around the paper like a school child causing Ophelia to roll her eyes.

As each attendee turned over their paper and slid it across the table to Matilda, she gathered them into a pile. Ophelia used the momentary distraction to snatch an almond cake.

Three suggested plays hung in the balance: a crowd-pleasing musical that had made waves twenty years before and was still hugely popular, a vintage comedy with rave reviews since its debut in 1920, and Macbeth—that cursed Scottish play that had caused chaos in professional theaters for centuries.

As the votes were being cast, Ophelia could not shake the feeling that the amateur dramatics society was setting in motion something far more consequential than a simple community theatrical production. The storm growled overhead like an ominous warning.

Imogen was drastically opposed to Shakespeare as it took a certain degree of talent she felt was missing from the amateur group. Was there anything worse than Shakespeare poorly executed? She let her eyes wander around the table; they were a rather motley crew.

The vicar's wife, Prudence Cresswell, stared at Matilda's solid hands counting the votes like a hawk watching a mouse, as if the result would decide the next king of England. Like Imogen, Pru was here as a stagehand; her nervous disposition did not lend itself to being the center of attention.

Celina Sutherland, the young librarian, was biting her lip. Her youth and classically pretty features made her a perfect fit for any female lead and Imogen was sure she had no desire to play an ugly witch.

Matilda cleared her throat and the murmuring quieted.

"We have a clear winner. *The Pirate's Fiancée* wins with seven votes."

The aging, dusty lights overhead cast shadows that emphasized the ripples of Reginald Tumblethorn's purple satin shirt, a bold but not unexpected choice that matched his peacock-print bow tie. Clapping enthusiastically, he leaned forward, his expression overly eager, clearly delighted at the potential the musical offered. Ophelia had no doubt he was angling for the role of the pirate.

She caught Pierre Ancien's eye. He was thinking the same thing and winked at her. Over the last few months, they had seen a lot of each other and were beginning to read one another's mind. What role would she cast him in?

"Can I look at those?" asked Mildred, indicating the votes with her eyes.

She does not believe Matilda! It was a thought that ruffled Imogen's feathers.

"Of course," responded Matilda with tight lips, handing over the pile. "Now, we need to start thinking about sets. Pierre and Reggie, can I count on you to help with those?"

"Of course," replied Pierre. "And I think we can recruit the Cleaver boys too."

Mildred's brows made a sharp 'v'. "Now that Peter is stepping out with that girl from Willowbrook, he might not be available."

It never ceased to amaze Imogen how Mildred knew *everything* about *everyone*.

"And Ophelia, you're here as our musician." She slid the music across the table. Ophelia took it with her sticky fingers. Though she was a retired professional violinist, her mother had been a piano teacher who made sure both her girls could play.

"Imogen, since you are a stagehand, you can help me with costuming."

"Right you are."

"Good! That's settled then." Matilda touched the bottom of her curled, white hair and looked around the circle. "We'll need more people than usual since there are several chorus numbers, so put the word out. We'll start auditions next Saturday."

"Who will be on the audition panel?" asked Patricia.

"I'll give it some thought but since this is a musical, prowess in that area will be considered." She pulled a stack of scripts from her bag and fanned them on the tabletop.

"You had already decided!" Mildred accused, the dead bird on her hat shaking with indignation.

"Not so, my bag is full of all the scripts," Matilda said, raising a bulky holdall from the floor.

Mildred merely grumbled and snatched a script.

As she left the building, Matilda pursed her lips as if holding back a smile.

"What?" Pierre asked.

"I bent the truth a little," she admitted in a whisper. "I do have the script of the comedy in my bag, but I didn't bother bringing the Shakespeare. Mildred was the one to propose it and the only one to vote for it."

A tiny woman with frizzy, blonde hair approached with a sparkle in her green eyes and humming a lively tune. "I'm so excited," she trilled. "I used to love acting at school in Manchester."

"We're very glad you decided to join us, Molly. How about that husband of yours?"

Her smile fell a notch, her bottom lip pulling into a shrug. "Eddie? He's a might clumsy for anything like this, I'm afraid. Those long legs and big feet have a habit of getting in the way."

"Is he handy?" asked Ophelia. "We need people to help create the sets."

Molly Sugden pushed out her lips in a pout as she considered the question. "He put up some new shelves in the shop." She flapped her hand at the wrist. "And they haven't fallen down yet!"

"Then he's hired," chuckled Matilda.

Molly walked away, waving over her shoulder. "I'll give him the good news."

"She seems nice," remarked Celina. "I thought the sweet shop might stay closed a little longer after the Fudgefords left." She refrained from mentioning why the Fudgefords had been forced to move.

"Oh, Molly is lovely!" said Imogen with feeling.

The twins had been one of the first to visit the new residents of the *Jolly Lolly*. Whether it was to satisfy their penchant for sweets, or their curiosity was still up for debate. They had been impressed with the way the new couple had rearranged the colorful confections as a kind of rainbow. Moving from shades of red all the way through to violet. Even the bell above the door had been polished to a cheerful shine. "Do you know Molly can guess your favorite sweet without being told?"

"Is that so," responded Celina.

"She got it right for both me and Ophelia. It's amazing."

Alice Puddingfield joined the group. "Trying out for the lead, Imogen?"

"Haha! Hardly! I'll stick to being behind the scenes, thank you."

"You'll try, won't you Celina?" continued Alice.

"I'm not the best singer … but, yes. I'll give it a go."

"Nonsense! You're one of the stronger singers in the choir," said Ophelia, who knew what she was talking about as choir director since the former one had landed in prison. "You'd be perfect. You can come to the cottage for singing lessons if you like."

Celina buttoned up her heavy coat and pulled out an umbrella. "Wouldn't that be inconvenient?"

"We're retired, ducky. What else do we have to do?" Pierre helped Ophelia into her coat.

"What about that new teacher, Miss Fairfax?" asked Imogen, snapping her handbag shut.

"She's great," replied Celina. "She's been into the library a few times and we've been for a drink at the pub. I was desperate for someone my own age to move into the village and she's been a godsend."

"Do you think she'd be game for some theatrics?" asked Matilda.

"I'll ask her. We're going out again tomorrow evening." She brandished the umbrella. "Now I have to brave the storm to get home to feed the cat. Cheerio!"

The rain had started before the meeting and continued steadily throughout. Imogen would have preferred snow.

"All done in here, Miss Butterworth?" asked the unassuming custodian, Rex Stout, large broom already in hand.

"Yes, thanks Rex."

"Speaking of animals, we should get back to feed Tiger. He'll scratch all the paint off the doorframe if we leave him too long."

Pierre held up Imogen's wool coat then offered his arms to both ladies. "You can 'old up your umbrellas and shield me from the rain." His delightful accent always made Imogen feel giggly. "Shall we go?"

They said goodbye to everyone left in the hall as Rex pinched one of the remaining cakes and began to clean the floor with long strokes of the broom. Then the threesome ventured out into the wet afternoon.

"The only good thing about February is March," said Ophelia, dodging puddles. "What part are you going to try out for, Pierre?"

"I don't think pirates are French. They're always English."

Ophelia was about to contradict him, but when she thought about it, he was right. "Well, the colonel certainly won't try out for it, which leaves Reggie, Des, Archie and the vicar."

They had a good laugh imagining Reverend Cresswell as the swashbuckling pirate, wooing the young heroine.

Reggie ran to catch up with them, an otter's fur coat kissing his ankles and an American cowboy hat on his head. "Isn't this exciting! I've always wanted to do a musical."

"Ten pounds says Mildred auditions for the lead role," Imogen muttered.

"Twenty says she demands to be assistant director," Ophelia countered.

Pierre shook his head. "You're both wrong. She will want to be the director AND the lead." His accent made even gossip sound charming. "But what interests me more is why our dear Mildred is so eager to perform Shakespeare. No one would come to see it."

"Well, Agatha Trumble was interested in Shakespeare too," Imogen reminded him. "That would have made two votes for Macbeth if she were still alive."

"Though I still mourn the headmistress's passing, I am glad that the only one in favor of Macbeth was Mildred."

"I played Shylock in a school play," said Reggie unexpectedly. "I can still remember the lines, you know. But I wasn't fond of the play. This is me." He peeled off and into the small corner shop. "Bye!"

Though the rain was still pelting the windows, they caught a glimpse of his elderly mother greeting him in her Victorian widow's cap, and Reggie turning to rearrange something in the eclectic shop window.

Harold Cleaver waved at them through the streaming panes at the butcher's and they nodded back, clutching their umbrellas.

Imogen stepped in a puddle as they crossed the road. "*Hot crumpets*! My foot's all wet."

"That's the ticket," replied Ophelia. "Hot crumpets by the fire."

"*And* that second almond cake that's in your pocket," accused Pierre with a chuckle.

"I couldn't let Alice's culinary perfection go to waste now, could I?"

The village green looked almost foggy through the heavy veil of precipitation as they traversed and crossed the bridge over the pond and onto their road. It was hard to see Badger's Hollow at all.

They scurried through the white arbor gate one at a time and hurried up the path.

Ruff, ruff!

Tiger was waiting at the window, his huge, furry face squashed against the glass in an expression of doggy betrayal. The excitable guard dog had been with them since their former librarian went to prison.

"Don't give me that look," Ophelia scolded as she unlocked the door. "We're not *that* late."

"'E is worse than my mother," Pierre chuckled, following them inside. "Always watching the clock."

Before they could stop him, Tiger jumped up at Pierre almost knocking him over. "Good to see you too, Tiger."

Imogen pulled at his collar and the dog turned, licking all over her face. "Haha. Down boy! Down!"

He slid past them to do his business outside and was back before they had closed the door, making for the warmth of the living room.

The heat from the embers of the morning fire spiraled in the grate and Ophelia threw on a couple of logs to feed it, stirring the remnants with the poker to create a new blaze.

"I'll get those crumpets and some butter and jam while the kettle is boiling." Imogen left the room as Pierre and Ophelia settled together on the sofa, wondering if the pair would make an announcement of any kind soon.

Finding the crumpets they had bought from the baker two days earlier, she laid them on a tray, catching a glimpse of the local honey they had purchased from Reggie. It was his hand drawn label of local flowers that had caused her to buy the pot. After lighting the oven and filling the old, battered kettle, she found the condiments and laid them on the tray with the honey.

Nudging the door, Tiger looked up from his position at Pierre's feet. Ophelia was just raising her head from Pierre's shoulder and Imogen wished she had taken more time preparing the light meal.

"Here we go," she said, casting around for the toasting fork. The flames of the resurrected fire licked the sides of the fire box. "I think the embers are hot enough."

"Please, allow me," said Pierre offering his hand.

Imogen pushed the first crumpet onto the prongs and Pierre moved to a chair by the fire to hold it in the dancing flames.

"It's just like watching Daddy," mused Ophelia with a lazy smile and Imogen's mind filled with a tumble of nostalgic memories. She leaned into the back of the chair, fingering the locket at her neck and allowing the past to wash over her for a precious moment.

As they watched Pierre expertly turn the crumpet in the flickering flames, Ophelia reflected on the meeting of the amateur dramatics society.

"I hope we won't have a battle of wills over this musical. I sometimes wish Mildred was less involved in all the workings of the village."

Mildred Chumbley had her finger in many pies. She was not only head bellringer, but also president of the women's institute and a member of the village council.

"Who do you think Matilda will ask to be on the auditioning committee?" asked Imogen. "Pierre, who usually helps with that?"

"Well, it *was* Agatha Trumble, Connie Featherstone and Douglas Horton Black in the past, so Matilda will 'ave to create a whole new crew." Agatha had died at the hands of a thief, and both Connie and Douglas were in prison for their crimes.

Pierre pulled a perfectly toasted crumpet from the flames and pointed it at Ophelia. "Since it is a musical, I bet it will be you two."

"That might be a nice change of pace," remarked Imogen.

A deep, infectious guffaw burst from deep in Pierre's chest.

"What?" asked Ophelia. "What's so funny?"

"If my assumption proves correct, you 'ave no idea what you are in for."

CHAPTER 2

Auditions and Ambitions

The sisters approached the village hall with some trepidation. Pierre's prediction had come true; Matilda had invited both sisters to be on the audition committee. But his amusement about the situation had given them cause for concern.

Though Saffron Weald was still in February's grip, the dreaded rain had stopped and the sun was making a timid effort at appearing through the gloom.

Ophelia placed her fingers on the handle of the village hall door and faced her sister. "Are you ready for this?"

Imogen's mouth turned down. "As I'll ever be."

They both took a deep breath and entered, coming face to face with a lively throng of eager actors. Matilda had placed posters all over the village announcing the play and audition times and her advertising had done the job.

"You're here!" Matilda's hat was off center and her cheeks a fire engine red. "It will just be the three of us since we won't be auditioning. No conflict of interest. Phew!" She fanned her face with a piece of paper. "I'm exhausted already."

"Excuse me," said Rex, sliding out the doors in his overalls and flat cap. "I'll be off for a bit, but I'll be back to clean up later."

As the twins took their seats, Matilda invited the hopeful actors to take their places in the chairs facing the stage.

"Right. Will all those of you trying out for the part of Philomena, the fiancée, please make for the wings. Oh—" A great deal of white hair from Matilda's bun had escaped and was curling around her sticky face. "I forgot. Ophelia, would you play the piano? I thought I'd planned everything but—" She shrugged both shoulders.

"Of course."

Grabbing the music from her bag, Ophelia made her way over to the out-of-tune-piano and waited for the first auditioner to appear center stage, a buxom girl of about fifteen with large front teeth and pretty eyes.

"Sally Pratt, isn't it?" asked Matilda. Imogen scribbled down the name. "Let's try the first aria. Page three, please."

Imogen watched as Ophelia turned to the correct page while trying to write the girl's name on another piece of paper. Her sister placed the pencil between her teeth while tapping out the opening bars of the intro.

Sally started out well but by the middle of the song she had gone flat and the audience of hopefuls were staring at each other or looking at the floor while the younger members were trying not to giggle.

"That will do! Thank you, Sally. Next!" cried Matilda.

Imogen placed an 'x' by Sally's name.

Celina Sutherland, the librarian, who had come to the cottage for a couple of voice lessons, shuffled out onto the stage looking more nervous than Imogen had ever seen her.

"Hello," she managed, gripping the music with both hands.

Matilda turned to Ophelia. "From the top, if you please."

Though Celina started out very quietly, by the middle of the piece, she was gaining her stride, hitting all the notes perfectly. Her tone was clear and pleasant which was perfect for the role of the innocent fiancée who is unaware that her new beau is, in fact, an infamous pirate.

Matilda waved her hands again. "Lovely, dear. That will be all.

Next!"

Imogen marked a large 'yes' by Celina's name.

Ophelia nearly fell off her piano bench when the next person to appear onstage was the highly conservative Patricia Snodgrass. The part was for a *young* woman. Patricia had to be at least forty.

"Patricia! What a lovely surprise," gasped Matilda failing to hide her confusion. She turned frantic eyes on Ophelia. "One more time, please."

Imogen had to purse her lips to avoid embarrassing herself and bent her head as if she were taking copious notes. Patricia's voice was unpolished and operatic. She did more quivering than a spotted warbler. Imogen placed a large 'x' by her name.

Before Patricia had even reached the zenith of the aria, Matilda cut her off. "Splendid! Splendid, Patricia! Jolly good effort. Next!"

A tiny, thin as a rail, young stranger stepped out from the wings. Imogen felt the urge to feed her a donut. Inching forward, the girl held the music at her side, biting her lip.

"Ah, Miss Fairfax," said Matilda. "Kitty, isn't it?"

So, *this* was the new primary school teacher. She worked at the school in Willowbrook but rented a little cottage in Saffron Weald. Flaming red hair set off emerald eyes and peachy skin. She wore a kilt and a handmade jumper that drowned her.

Kitty turned to leave.

"Where are you going?" asked Matilda.

"I've changed my mind. I'm not that good at singing. I'll try for the chorus." Her strong brogue was from the area of Birmingham.

Matilda was not having it. "Wait! Since you're here, why don't you give it a go?"

Miss Fairfax shook her head and wrinkled her nose. "I don't know …"

Matilda nodded at Ophelia who played the intro again.

Suddenly, the tiny woman belted out the notes in a rich, mature sound that stopped all the chattering in the hall. Ophelia shot a meaningful look at Imogen. Here was true talent.

This time, Matilda did not stop Ophelia and Miss Fairfax sang the aria in its entirety. When she finished, the hall erupted into spontaneous applause.

Heat crept up Kitty's neck but she could not hold back a shy smile. Imogen placed a big 'yes' next to her name and several asterisks.

"You're very talented," gushed Matilda. "Bravo!"

As Kitty slipped off the stage, several of the waiting performers surrounded her.

"That was wonderful!" Sally Pratt clasped her hands together. "I had no idea you could sing like that, Miss Fairfax."

Kitty's face nearly matched her fiery red hair. "Oh... it's nothing really. Just something I did for fun at school and then in teacher training college." She tugged at the sleeve of her oversized jumper, clearly wishing she could disappear inside it.

"Nothing?" Patricia Snodgrass's eyebrows shot up. "My dear, with a voice like that, you could have pursued a career as a professional actress!"

"No, no." Kitty shook her head vigorously. "I much prefer teaching the little ones. Though," she added with a small smile, "they're a far more demanding audience than this lot."

The group of ladies laughed, but Imogen noticed how Kitty edged away from the attention, finding a quiet corner with Celina to watch the remaining auditions. She made a mental note that their talented new teacher might need some coaxing to accept the leading role, assuming Matilda offered it to her.

Matilda asked if there were any others auditioning for the part but no one stepped forward. Ophelia had the impression that even if there were others who had hopes for the part, they had changed their minds during Miss Fairfax's performance.

"Alright then. Moving on to ..." she looked at her list. "The pirate, Captain Leopold 'Lucky' Blackwood."

Several men got up from the audience and made their way to the stairs that led up to the stage. The music for the pirate was much more campy than the aria for the fiancée and several of the men made a pretty good job of it, including one of the local farmers called Jones. Then Reggie appeared onstage. Today, he wore striped, green trousers and an emerald waistcoat.

"Lalalala." He cleared his throat.

"Are you ready, dear?" asked Matilda looking at her watch.

He nodded and Ophelia banged out the intro. The sound that came out of his mouth was like that of a cat being dragged backwards through a trumpet. He warbled several octaves too high, then plunged into depths that made the floorboards vibrate. His rendition of the pirate's swagger song included random falsetto leaps that caused several audience members to flinch in pain.

"Yo ho ho and a bottle of RUM!" He pirouetted dramatically, the striped trousers a blur as he spun. The last note emerged as a sort of strangled yodel that hung in the horrified silence.

Imogen closed her mouth, eyes wide.

"That was ... certainly unique," Matilda managed.

"I've been practicing," Reggie announced proudly, either oblivious to, or choosing to ignore, the way several people were discreetly snickering.

Reggie had the innocence of a child though he was around forty. Sheltered by an over-protective mother whose husband died young, he rarely left the little village. Imogen was of the opinion that Reggie was immune to societal expectations. She was sure he truly believed he had executed an exceptional audition.

"I can tell," replied Matilda. Looking past him, she asked, "Is there anyone else?"

Grinning from ear to ear, Reggie passed Desmond Ale, the friendly publican, as he walked off stage.

Des, a widower, had suffered more than his fair share of setbacks in life but still managed to maintain his gift for making everyone who walked through the doors of his pub feel welcome. Add to those gifts the fact that every older woman in the village felt a certain motherly instinct toward him and he was one of the village's most popular residents.

Imogen awaited with hopeful expectation, familiar with Des's rich, deep voice from the village choir.

She was not disappointed.

Des came alive on stage, his innate charm perfect for the role of the comedic pirate. His powerful voice belted out the song with infectious enthusiasm as he spread wide his arms as if inviting the entire audience to join in the adventure.

The other hopefuls cheered when he finished.

"Marvelous, Des. Marvelous." Matilda checked her list again. "Thank you, gentlemen. Now, the fiancée's mother, Prudentia Bottomley-Blythe."

Horrified when Mildred Chumbley emerged from the crowd of hopefuls, Imogen exchanged an anxious glance with her sister who laughed and mimed counting money. The play was a comedic musical; not something that sprang to mind when thinking of Mildred.

Alice Puddingfield was the first to try. She did an adequate job and since the song was amusing and music-hallesque, a brilliant voice was not absolutely vital. Surprisingly, Patricia Snodgrass tried out for this role too, but her operatic tone clashed horribly with the upbeat music and Imogen was glad when her audition was over.

Ophelia nearly fell off her piano bench when the new headmistress, Judith Rutherford, stepped out onto the stage. She had moved to the village six months before as an emergency replacement, and once she had grappled the small school into order, had thrown herself into village life. Her audition was brilliant. She was head and shoulders above the rest and even sang with the slightly cheeky tone necessary for the part. Imogen scribbled a large 'yes' next to her name and a constellation of asterisks.

The final person trying out for the role of the mother was the petite new confectioner, Molly Sugden. She had taken off her apron in favor of a pretty dress that flattered her shape, and a stylish hat.

Having never heard her sing, Ophelia was astonished when

Molly performed the song like a pro. She was obviously no stranger to community theater. They would have a difficult time choosing who should perform *this* role.

Halfway through the chorus auditions, a commotion from stage left, drew everyone's attention. Tommy Fletcher, one of the more rambunctious twelve-year-olds, had decided the heavy velvet curtains would make an excellent climbing frame.

"Tommy! Get down from there this instant!" Matilda half-rose from her chair, hat now completely adrift.

"But I've got a great view from up here!" Tommy swung gleefully, causing the rickety curtain rail to emit an ominous creak. His best friend, Collin Shelton, inspired by Tommy's daring, grabbed the other curtain. "Bet I can climb higher than you, Tom!"

"Oh, good grief," muttered Ophelia, abandoning the piano to help Matilda deal with the crisis. The curtains swayed dangerously as the two boys scaled higher, sending down clouds of dust that had several auditioners sneezing. Des, still in pirate mode, stepped forward.

"Ahoy there, ye young scalawags! Those be the captain's personal sails you're aclimbing! Any man caught tampering with them walks the plank!"

Tommy, caught between showing off and being impressed by Des's impromptu performance, lost his grip. The curtain swung wildly, wrapping around him like a dusty cocoon while Collin, trying to avoid the same fate, jumped – landing directly in Patricia Snodgrass's lap.

"Well," said Matilda, once order had been restored and Tommy had been extracted from his velvet prison, "I think we can safely say those curtains need a good beating before opening night."

The rest of the auditions passed with only one little boy vomiting. It was efficiently cleared up by Rex. But by the end of the afternoon, Imogen had a sharp pain behind her eye and was desperate for a cup of tea. Matilda slumped into the seat next to her, face still flaming red and tiny dots of perspiration scattered across her forehead.

"Well done!" said Imogen with honesty. "You should get a raise."

Matilda only moved her eyes. "Haha. Double my salary and it's still nothing." She bubbled over with merry laughter.

Ophelia joined them with a large sigh. "That was a lot of work. I need a nap."

"Don't we all," agreed Matilda. "I instructed Daisy to lay on a spread for the three of us at *Thyme for Tea*. Please, be my guests."

"You don't have to ask *me* twice." Ophelia was already slipping on her coat.

As they moved to leave, Mildred cornered them. "I hope you won't show any favoritism in choosing the parts." Her ugly grimace was poisonous as sulphuric acid. "I think there were some clear winners here today." She adjusted her hat and turned on her heel.

"What did *she* want?" Pierre approached, his eye on the departing Mildred.

"I reckon she fancies herself a star," snickered Ophelia.

CHAPTER 3

Doilies and Discussions

T hyme for Tea was a quaint, distinctly feminine tea shop on the high street, with huge, crocheted doilies for tablecloths. The tables themselves were a collection of antiques that looked as though they had been gathered from a dozen different estate sales—some round, some square, no two exactly alike. Each was paired with different vintage chairs, all painted in pink, and fitted with plump floral cushions. As usual it was crowded with ladies from the village.

"I thought we could discuss the parts in private." Matilda led them through to the back of the store and up the stairs to her living quarters. The sitting room was small and looked like a pink monster had thrown up over everything. Beyond the overwhelming decor, Matilda's living room bore all the comfortable untidiness of a space that was actually lived in; a half-finished piece of knitting spilled from a basket beside her Queen Anne chair, needles thrust through a ball of cream wool. Dog-eared scripts from past productions were stacked on several surfaces, and former teacups had left pale rings on the side tables, despite the ever-present doilies' attempts to prevent them. Her theatrical past peeked through everywhere – a prop sword hung as a wall decoration, costume jewelry draped over a mirror's corner, and a collection of show programs fanned out on a bookshelf. A music stand in one corner held the score for *The Pirate's Fiancée*, its pages already weathered from frequent consultation.

"Have a seat."

The twins sank into a sofa that reminded Ophelia of the mother bear's furniture in *Goldilocks*. Matilda chose the Queen Anne chair with doilies on each arm and rang a little bell that sat on a delicate side table. She patted her flyaway hair while picking up a clipboard. "I think we can all agree that most of the parts had a clear winner—"

Daisy bumped into the room holding a tray laden with tea and pastries. Imogen's mouth began to water.

"Shall I be mother?" Matilda dropped the clipboard on her lap and was already pouring tea into the cups.

Imogen took the cup she was offered, and placing it on her knee, reached for a warm sticky bun.

"As I was saying, there's no doubt in my mind that Des should get the part as the pirate, Lucky Blackwood. Agreed?"

The twins simply nodded with full mouths as steam rose from their cups.

Placing the tea pot back on the tray, Matilda asked, "I'm leaning toward Kitty Fairfax as the fiancée, even though she has that strong Brummie accent. My only other reservation is that I have never seen her act."

Imogen spoke through a mouthful she was swallowing. "She has such a beautiful voice people will forgive any bad acting, and anyway, its comedy. A little hamming it up will go a long way. I'd be happy to ask if she can do other accents or tone it down a bit."

Matilda fiddled with the doily on the arm of her chair. "Would you? I'd be most grateful. Let's put that assignment on hold for the time being, then. Celina would be good in that part too. Now, the mother. It's another obvious choice, if you ask me. Molly Sugden. Again, I don't know if she can act."

Ophelia dabbed at her lips with a napkin. "Molly mentioned to me she had done amateur theater in Manchester."

"That reminds me, Kitty mentioned she had been in

productions at school and training college." Imogen beamed over her tea.

"Fantastic." Matilda reached for a cream bun with one hand while writing on the clipboard with the other. "I think we'll put Celina in as the fiancée's best friend for now. The other ladies can be in the chorus."

"What shall we do with Reggie? I had no idea he was so … energetic." Imogen grinned at Matilda as she dug into a bun.

Matilda's fingers drummed against her teacup as she considered the delicate subject. "Bless him. What he lacks in talent he makes up for in enthusiasm. He's tried out for the lead in the last five plays. The good thing is, he doesn't get upset when he doesn't get it. Not like some others I could mention."

"Oh?" Ophelia leaned forward.

Matilda brushed crumbs off her heavy skirt. "You heard Mildred. She's a disaster, so she never gets a lead role, but she always lets me have it."

Imogen put her cup on the coffee table. "She doesn't sing like that in the choir. I know because she stands next to me."

"I have long suspected that she's a *follower*," said Ophelia.

Matilda stirred another sugar into her tea. "What do you mean?"

"Well, there are leaders – those who are confident of the notes – and followers, those who are less confident and wait for the person next to them to hit the note first. That's how Mildred rolls. So, when she's singing solo, she's always a little off key."

Imogen tried crossing her legs but found it too challenging on the soft sofa and almost lost her cup. "What part *will* you give her?"

"She can sing in the chorus too. If she's a follower as you say, that's the best place for her."

Ophelia gripped the arm of the couch and pulled herself forward. "Back to Reggie. Can he be one of the other pirates?"

"Yes, that will do, and we'll find him the most outlandish costume we have. That will make him happy." She bubbled over with laughter.

"And the other pirates?" asked Imogen, looking at the multitude of cat pictures on the walls.

"All those who auditioned for the lead. There are four other pirates in the script." She patted her hair again.

"I assume we're casting the children as the townsfolk?" Imogen tried edging forward in her seat.

"I do have a policy of giving all those who audition, a part in the show. It takes a great deal of nerve to get up there and sing in front of everyone and I think that kind of grit should be rewarded, don't you?"

"*Bloomin' biscuits*, yes! Absolutely!" agreed Ophelia.

Imogen pulled at the waistband of her skirt. "Judith was incredible too. I had no idea she was such a showman. Is there a solo part for her?"

Matilda clapped her hands. "I almost forgot. The chaperone. She's a woman of a certain age who accompanies the fiancée everywhere and sings a couple of duets. What do you think of putting Farmer Jones in the role of the admiral who courts Mrs. Bottomley-Blythe?"

The twins chuckled in tandem. "Perfect!"

Matilda placed the clipboard and pencil on the coffee table and took another cream bun. "I think that's all the main parts sorted. If you can just find out about Kitty for me?" She looked up with a wrinkled brow.

"Of course." Imogen pointed to a photograph of a much younger Matilda dressed as a French courtier with a beauty spot on her upper lip. "Is that you?"

Matilda put a hand to her chest with closed eyes and pinched lips. "Can you believe it? Once society finally realized that acting was not an inherently corrupting force and destructive to the morals of those who participated in it, I was all in. Though it took some persuading to get my parents to agree. I grew up in Longmanshire, on a farm. My father couldn't understand why I wanted to act and worried for my virtue, which was a laugh because those in our local theater group were all over sixty! They were thrilled when I joined. I got all the leading roles, you know. And thus began my love of the theater." She drew a finger across her brow. "When I moved to Saffron Weald, the amateur dramatics society was all but dying out, and they couldn't get anyone to come and watch the plays. That all changed when I took over."

Ophelia remembered attending a show when they had first moved back to the village. It had been standing room only.

"Did your father ever soften his views?"

Matilda pushed some wisps of hair out of her eyes. "I had to drag him to the first show I was in, but after that he was my biggest champion, God rest his soul."

"And the rest of your family?"

Matilda's mood dipped and she twisted a loose thread on her cardigan sleeve, rolling it between her thumb and forefinger as she spoke. "Well, we have our ups and downs. My sister June was very supportive, but Janice couldn't get a grip on her jealousy. She envied me the limelight. But then she got married and had four children. You'd think that would balance the field since I never married, but no. Still makes underhand remarks and the like. Unfortunately, we haven't spoken in several years."

Using the arm of the couch for leverage, Imogen inched forward. "Oh, I'm sorry to hear that."

"Don't be. It's her fault. The minute she makes a move in the right direction I shall reignite the relationship. She's just being petty."

"No brothers?" Imogen had always wanted a brother, but her mother had suffered during the delivery of the twins so much that the doctors had recommended she never give birth again.

Matilda's smile returned. "Morris. We were ever so close as kids, but he had wanderlust. Left home at sixteen to see the world. Crushed my father who wanted him to take over the farm. We had to sell it when my parents died. That's how I bought the shop." Her eyes took on a faraway look. "Morris pops in every now and again without announcement. It's always lovely to see him."

Imogen struggled to get off the couch. "Can you give me the

key to the costume cabinet? I'd like to have a look and see what we have and what we need to make. And I bet some of the old ones could do with a good wash."

"Without a doubt." Matilda rose and went to a sideboard where she opened a little drawer and pulled out a key. "Here you go."

Imogen put it in her handbag.

"Do you need us to do anything with the scenery?" asked Ophelia. "I have to warn you, neither of us has any talent in that area."

Matilda quirked her brow. "What Reggie lacks in acting and singing talent, he more than makes up for with his art. Did you know he's a brilliant painter?"

Ophelia recalled the stacks of notebooks containing sketches and paintings of birds Reggie's mother had shown them in the summer. "Yes. I understand he's even won awards."

"It's true. He designs all our backdrops and scenery."

Ophelia pulled on her gloves. "We'll tootle off, then. Thanks for the tea."

"It was my pleasure." Matilda showed them to the door. "By the way, I keep all the assignments secret until I post the final casting on the door of the village hall." She closed the door as she left a parting thought. "And I wish you both the best of luck avoiding Mildred."

CHAPTER 4

Accents and Accusations

Since the next day dawned bright and clear, the twins thought it the perfect opportunity to visit Kitty Fairfax while taking Tiger for a walk. She lived in one of the old laborers' cottages just off the high street that formed a crescent by the village green.

All the buildings in Saffron Weald, except for the post office that was a converted smith barn, and Stirling Manor, were made of wattle and daub construction, the whitewash of the plaster contrasting starkly with the black timbers. Twelve cottages made up the crescent, cradling the village green like cupped hands and all sharing one vast thatch roof.

In the late winter sun, the weathered roofs resembled the tousled fur of sleeping cats. Smoke curled from crooked chimneys, carrying the sweet scent of apple wood, while in front of the cottages, the first brave snowdrops pushed through the frost-hardened earth.

Each front door was painted a different color, and the cheer of warm fires glowed behind the tiny windows. Tiger's ears perked as the church clock marked the quarter hour.

As they crunched across the frost-bitten green, Kitty's yellow front door in their sights, Mildred intercepted them.

Flaming fiddles!

"Has the audition committee decided on the parts?" Mildred bobbed forward like a pigeon, her head pitching as her beady eyes switched between the sisters. Ophelia tensed at the sight, while Imogen tightened her grip on Tiger's lead, giving him the signal to sit. The dog watched Mildred with curiosity but made no move to sniff her.

"You know we can't comment on that, Mildred. The list will be up soon enough. A little patience goes a long way."

Mildred glared at Tiger through narrowed eyes. "I deserve the part of the mother, you know. I've tried out for many lead roles over the last few years and not got any of them. It's my turn."

Mildred and Ophelia had often sparred since the twins return to the village. She spoke up. "Then you are aware that parts are awarded solely on merit."

"I was as good as any of the others," Mildred spat. "And that headmistress is no better than she should be."

This accusation was outrageous and made Ophelia's blood boil. The new headmistress was brilliant at her job and had revolutionized the archaic methods of discipline at the little school. Ophelia decided it would be better to let Imogen continue the conversation in case she said anything she might later regret.

"Now, now," said Imogen, patting the dog's head to cool her own temper. "Let's not bandy about malicious gossip that might ruin someone's reputation."

The villagers said Mildred could smell scandal the way others smelled rain coming, and that she patrolled the village as a self-appointed moral guardian. These days, she reserved particular venom for women who stepped beyond their traditional roles, as if each small act of independence was a personal affront.

"It's not gossip; I saw it with my own eyes through the school windows. She was wearing *trousers* and teaching the girls to throw punches."

Even if this were true, it hardly led to the conclusion that Judith Rutherford was a hussy.

"I'm sure there's a reasonable explanation and I beg you

not to slander the poor woman. As a newcomer we should be welcoming her, not painting her with a scarlet letter."

"It's just not right that women wear men's clothing." Mildred was a product of the last century and as such, clung stubbornly to Victorian sensibilities. But the world was changing around her, and more and more young women were choosing to wear trousers for daily tasks such as brisk walks, riding and just for fun. Ophelia hailed the practical fashion, not just for its utility, but as a modest alternative to the scandalously short skirts becoming so popular.

"They are not sporting *men's* pantaloons, Mildred. These new trousers are cut for a woman's curved shape."

Mildred tutted with disgust before asking, "Where are you going?"

The twins shared a look. "Just taking Tiger for his daily constitutional," said Ophelia, noting to herself that it was none of Mildred's business.

"Umm, well." Mildred turned to leave and the twins let out a sigh. "I expect to be on that list," she hissed over her shoulder.

By mutual agreement, the twins bypassed Kitty's house until Mildred was well out of the way.

"That woman!" wailed Ophelia as they traversed the green again.

"I know, lovey. Mildred is one of those souls sent to try us. But I think she's gone." Though Imogen would not put it past her to spy on them.

They approached the yellow front door and knocked, Tiger sniffing the corners.

"Hello!" The spindly Kitty bent down to run her hands through Tiger's thick mane. "What a beauty!"

"How do you feel about dogs in the house?" asked Ophelia, before stepping forward.

"Luv it. Grew up with a whole pack." Ophelia noted the strong, throaty 'k' sound of the accent of the city of Birmingham. "Would you like to come in?"

They had been in one of these miniature cottages before, but

Imogen was still surprised by just how tiny they were; the halls barely wide enough for two people to pass each other, and the stairs climbing at a dizzying angle.

"Come on through." Kitty pushed open the door to a pocket-sized parlor. "I'll put the kettle on."

Tiger seemed to fill the whole room.

"Lay down, boy."

Two well-used armchairs hugged the narrow, cast-iron fireplace which currently kicked out a vigorous heat. Tiger lay right next to it while each twin took a chair, wondering where Kitty would sit.

"Here we are." Kitty returned holding a stool. "It's so luvely having visitors."

"How are you settling in?"

Kitty had started at the school in Willowbrook at the beginning of the school year, staying in a rented room with one of the farmers' families. But the arrangement was only temporary and she had found the little cottage in Saffron Weald during the Christmas break. As far as Imogen could see, there were no personal items around the parlor or pictures on the walls.

"I still have some unpacked boxes that me mam sent me. Between school and marking papers I don't have a lot 'a time."

"And how do you get to your school from here?" asked Ophelia.

Kitty softly laid a hand on Tiger's huge head. He looked over his shoulder at her touch. "I ride me bike. I'm very glad we haven't had too much snow. Don't know what I'd do then." No wonder the girl was so painfully thin.

Ophelia opened her coat in the heat. "There's a sporadic bus service but it might not start early enough for you, and a very reliable taxi service out of Parkford. But you might also be able to find the odd ride with someone from the village."

"I'll cross that bridge when I come to it." A smile took over Kitty's whole face elevating it from pleasant to beautiful.

The kettle screamed. "Excuse me a min."

Tiger stirred and Imogen put a calming hand on his back.

Ophelia looked around the bleak room. "I'm sure Pierre would be more than happy to give her a ride on rainy mornings. He's good like that."

"You should mention it to him."

This particular cottage had been the home of the late Widow Clark, who had not only been born in the cottage, but raised six boys in it and buried a husband. The odor of the former occupant still clung to the walls. The whole place needed a good airing which would not happen until the spring brought warmer weather in a few weeks.

"Here we are." Kitty held a large tray with the tea things. Tiger lifted his snout with interest. "Can you?" She tipped her head to a rickety table in the corner and Imogen jumped up to get it.

As Kitty poured, Ophelia observed, "I should imagine Meadowshire is a far cry from Birmingham."

The girl lifted her wild mane of auburn locks and Ophelia thought she noticed a slight wince as she lifted her arm. *Over doing it on the bike.* "You could say that."

"Do you miss it?"

Kitty pursed her lips. "The truth is, I've come here to heal a broken heart."

Imogen was always up for a good love story. "Ahh, lovey. We understand that such things are very personal, but if you'd like to talk about it, we're both excellent listeners."

She handed them mismatched cups with chips around the edges.

"He went to school with me but was always getting into trouble. Why are we drawn to that?"

Imogen's Wilf had been a fine upstanding young man, and the boys Ophelia had walked out with were good country boys, but they both knew that rebels had a certain allure.

Imogen touched Kitty's arm. "Is that why you left?"

"No. I got a scholarship to teacher training college," she said, poking at a small hole in her worn skirt. "First in my family to go to college. Dad worked the foundry, mum took in washing.

They were that proud." Her smile turned wistful. "But Jack—that was his name—he worked the docks in Sherborne. He'd write these letters full of home news, about the pub and his mates and our old haunts. Then when I'd visit, wearing my new clothes and talking about Piaget and Locke, his eyes would go dark. Last Christmas he said, 'You're not our Kitty anymore, are you? All fancy ideas and big dreams.'" She blinked hard. "Two weeks later, he was walking out with Jane Boggs. Her dad owns the pub, see, and she knows her place, as Jack put it." She looked out the grimy window. "I suppose I *had* changed. I knew the world was bigger than Sherborne. But I still luved him." She took an absentminded sip of her tea and cringed, reaching for the sugar. "He thought I was better than him. He said he couldn't marry a girl who was so clever."

"Wounded pride," said Ophelia nodding her head. "Men are often intimidated by intellectually strong women."

"Something like that. Anyway, when he proposed to Jane Boggs, I ran away." Her eyes were shining. "Took the job here."

Ophelia patted her hand. "You're better off without him, ducky. It wouldn't have worked. He'd have held you back."

Kitty dropped her head.

"You were marvelous in your audition," exclaimed Imogen trying to brighten the gloomy atmosphere. "Simply wonderful. We were all very impressed."

Kitty brightened. "You were? I sang in the school chorus and had small parts in school plays, and such."

"Oh, yes. True talent, Kitty. But, um, we were wondering, did you ever have parts with accents?"

The shine in her green eyes became a twinkle. "Are you saying my Brummie accent wouldn't work for the pirate's fiancée?" She had said the words in almost perfect King's English.

Ophelia's shoulders began to shake as tears of mirth dribbled down her cheeks.

"You got us!" laughed Imogen. "Oh, very good, lovey. Very good."

"I have a knack for all kinds of accents," Kitty said in the country twang of Meadowshire. "It's a gift." She finished in the hard cockney of London.

"It certainly is! Well, as representatives of the audition committee, we would like to offer you the part of the fiancée."

"Are you kidding?" Kitty's eyes now grew wide with astonishment.

Ophelia was still incapacitated by her silent laughter.

"We're completely serious. We'll report back to Matilda and she'll post the cast list tomorrow on the door of the hall."

Through the smudged window, the twins caught a glimpse of Mildred's hideous, navy hat bobbing past, and though neither mentioned it, both felt a chill that had nothing to do with the winter air outside. Tiger's ears pricked up and a low growl rumbled in his chest – he had always been an excellent judge of character.

The village post office sat a little way off from the other shops on the high street and still bore traces of its history as the smithy's barn with massive oak beams that lined the ceiling. If you breathed in deeply, village folklore had it that you could still smell the old forge's ashes. When the twins entered, the post mistress, Patricia Snodgrass, stood at the counter arranging stamps.

"Just looking for more stationary," said Ophelia as she waved to Patricia. The twins slipped between the two aisles of paper, pens and rulers as the bell above the door rang.

"Mildred," said Patricia in an even tone.

"You'll never guess what I just saw at that school," Mildred announced, not bothering with the usual pleasantries.

The twins, hidden by a structural post, remained silent.

"And what would that be?" asked Patricia in a bored tone.

"That new headmistress, teaching girls to fight! In trousers, no less!" Each word dripped with judgment. "Whatever next? Teaching them to smoke cigarettes and drive motorcars?"

The twins locked eyes, hidden from view.

Patricia did not rise to the bait. "Seems logical to wear something practical if you're teaching students to fight."

"Why do our girls need to learn that? It's unladylike." Mildred's voice could have curdled milk. "Mark my words, Miss Rutherford will fill those girl's heads with all sorts of modern ideas. How are they ever going to find husbands?"

Ophelia's eyes turned to slits but when she made a move, Imogen grabbed her arm, whispering. "She's not worth the effort, lovey."

"But she's slandering that poor woman's good name," Ophelia hissed back.

"From what I know of Judith, she has broad shoulders. Hold your tongue. It won't end well."

"There seem to be more than a few of us in Saffron Weald that never found husbands holding onto the old ways," retorted Patricia. Ophelia wanted to cheer.

"Well, I didn't come in here to be insulted," threw back Mildred.

"Why *did* you come in?" asked Patricia.

"I need to mail this."

The twins heard something being pushed across the counter.

"That will be seven pence."

"That's daylight robbery," gasped Mildred.

"You can take it up with his Majesty." Patricia was in fine form.

They heard the cash register open and close then the bell jangle on the door like it was going to fall off.

They emerged.

"Bravo!" said Ophelia. "Mildred needed taking down a peg or two."

Patricia pushed a hand through her graying hair. "Look, I'm certainly not perfect where gossip is concerned, but that woman is the absolute limit."

"None of us is perfect in that department, but you defended Judith admirably," responded Ophelia with gusto.

"If that woman isn't careful, she will cross the wrong person," declared Patricia, eyes on the door.

CHAPTER 5

The Cast List

Matilda had asked the twins to post the cast list. She claimed she had urgent business in Parkford, but the twins wondered if she was just thankful to have someone else to take the brunt of the complaints.

As they stood by the village hall doors with their hammer and nail, people emerged from every direction, jostling to see over their shoulders, pressing closer and closer with whispered questions and craning necks.

"Please stand back," said Ophelia her voice climbing an octave with desperation. The crowd pressed so close she could feel their breath on her neck – there wasn't room to swing a cat let alone a hammer. "I don't want anyone to get hurt."

The inner circle moved barely an inch, boots scraping on the frozen ground.

Imogen held the paper in place, corner fluttering in the wind, while Ophelia positioned the nail. She drew back the hammer, acutely aware of watching eyes, before knocking the nail smartly on the head. Unfortunately, it bent sideways with a sad little ping.

"*Blazing bagpipes!*" Her cheeks flushed as someone snickered.

"Here, let me do it," offered Des, appearing at her left shoulder.

She dropped a second nail into his palm. He drove it home with one practiced strike and the twins ducked instinctively out of the way as the crowd surged forward, elbows digging and heads bobbing to get a good view.

Cast List for the Pirate's Fiancée

1. *Captain Leopold "Leo" Blackwood*   *Desmond Ale*
2. *Fiancée – Philomena Bottomley-Blythe*   *Kitty Fairfax*
3. *Lavinia – the best friend*   *Celina Sutherland*
4. *Mrs. Prudentia Bottomley-Blythe*   *Molly Sugden*
5. *Chaperone*   *Judith Rutherford*
6. *Admiral Bluster*   *Farmer Jones*
7. *Ladies' chorus*   *Every lady/girl who auditioned*
8. *Pirates' chorus*   *Every man/boy who auditioned*

It took only seconds for the moans and groans of disappointment amidst the shrieks of excitement. Job done, the twins quickly made for home, but Mildred was too fast and grabbed Imogen by the sleeve.

"I see I was overlooked again."

Ophelia stared at Mildred's grip as though her gaze were a hot iron capable of burning flesh. Mildred reluctantly withdrew her hand.

"We are not obliged to explain anything, but since you insist, you have to admit that Kitty, Molly and Judith are extraordinarily talented. It would have been criminal not to cast them in the lead roles."

Mildred grumbled something into her collar.

Ophelia could not help herself. "By the way. You need to use the tweezers on your chin. Tata!"

They scurried away as Mildred's hand flew to the pesky whiskers.

Since it was on their way home, they pushed into *Pierre's Antiques* in case Mildred accosted them again.

"Bonjour!" Pierre examined their flushed cheeks and tight jaws. "But you look like you're soldiers arriving 'ome from battle."

Ophelia kissed his cheek. "We just put up the cast list."

"Was that today?"

She swatted his arm. "You know full well it was."

"And Matilda made *you* do it?"

"She had business in Parkford," replied Imogen.

He grinned. "That's funny. I just saw her slipping into the pub."

"*Hot crumpets!* We've been had."

"'Ave an 'eart. Matilda 'as done it for the past seven years. She was due for a break."

Ophelia chuckled. "I suppose she was."

He checked his beautiful gold pocket watch. "Let me give you some tea as compensation." He walked to the back of the store and they followed him up the stairs to his apartment.

Pierre's private quarters wrapped around them like a Continental embrace. The furniture, the lamps and all the soft furnishings, were utterly French. As an antique dealer, he was able to track down authentic French items, and together with his innate flair for design, the whole place made you feel as if you had stepped into the finest French salon.

Imogen settled herself on a bergère chair, leaving the sofa to the courting couple. "Have you started on the scenery yet?"

"We 'ave our first planning meeting tonight. I offered to 'ave it 'ere, but Reggie insisted on 'olding the meeting at 'is place since Mrs. Tumblet'orn is feeling under the weather."

Reggie's mother had a delicate constitution brought on by her husband's death and her desire to join him. Only her love for her only child, Reggie, prevented her from slipping through the veil to meet her husband on the other side.

Ophelia glanced at the *boudeuse* loveseat but settled for the linen cabriole sofa as Pierre left for the kitchen. "Is Reggie as gifted with scenery as he is at capturing birds on paper?"

Pierre popped his head around the door. "Oh, yes. Do you not remember the play you saw when you first arrived back in Saffron Weald?"

"The comedy?"

"Yes. That was all Reggie's work."

At the time they had paid little attention to the backdrops for the play, but looking back, Ophelia had to agree they were pretty magnificent for a small community like theirs.

"'E is so talented, that at times we need to scale back 'is vision somewhat, as 'is ideas are somewhat ambitious for our limited resources."

"Is he any good at the woodworking side of things?" she called out as various noises erupted from the kitchen.

"'Old on!"

Even the paintings on the walls, framed with gold gilt, were French and Imogen suspected they were worth a pretty penny.

"There!" Pierre reappeared. "We'll just wait for the water to boil." As a Frenchman, Pierre preferred coffee, the stronger the better, but he knew his English friends preferred their national drink and he acquiesced to the tradition, though he still took his without milk.

"Where were we?"

Ophelia thought of her failure with the nail, earlier. "I was asking if Reggie was handy with a hammer."

Pierre closed his eyes and snorted. "Reggie 'as no clue with tools. 'E draws the outline on the wood and Des and I, and sometimes the Cleaver boys, cut it out. 'E would end up losing a finger if 'e tried."

"A bit like Ophelia at the village hall." Imogen told Pierre about how Des had rescued them.

"Des is very 'andy. I suppose you 'ave to be if you run a pub."

Ophelia slid closer to Pierre. "So, some of you cut it out and then Reggie paints the scene?"

"Exactement! We, 'ow do you say, *appliquer* the paint? Slat?" Pierre's English was impeccable but every now and again the word escaped him.

"Slap. Slap on some paint."

"That's the word. We put on a base and then Reggie does 'is magic."

"He didn't get a main part. Will he mind?" asked Imogen, as the kettle began to sing and Pierre arose.

He knitted his brow. "No! I think 'e likes to audition to get an opportunity to sing solo. I believe 'e 'as no expectations. I imagine 'is performance was … eccentric, non?"

"I'm guessing you've experienced one of his auditions," chuckled Ophelia.

"Oh, yes!" he said, slipping back into the kitchen.

As a master horologist, Pierre's walls also showcased two of his finest pieces. Ophelia's eyes drifted over the two familiar clocks she had come to love: the first featuring three naked, brass cherubs, their perfectly formed limbs straining as they held an orb above their heads, and the second, an elegant French bracket clock with its white enamel face and blue steel hands, nestled in an elaborate tortoiseshell veneer case with a matching bracket.

But today, something new caught her eye. An automaton clock she had not seen before sat on top of Pierre's gorgeous walnut cabinet. She wandered over to examine the new arrival and marveled at the intricacy of its design – a royal elephant rendered in exquisite detail, bearing a gilded throne on its back, upon which sat a prince in all his regal splendor. The miniature clock face itself was so artfully integrated into the design that it nearly disappeared, as if timekeeping were only secondary to the masterpiece's beauty.

"Is that new?" asked her sister.

"I think so."

Pierre returned with the tea and cakes and seeing Ophelia admiring his new clock, explained, "Isn't it lovely? I got it from an estate auction in Parkford. I could tell it 'ad been broken for years but I got it working again and decided to keep it. I displayed it in the shop for a few days and now it is mine to enjoy in private."

"Oh, I would too," agreed Ophelia coming back to the settee.

"You asked if I 'ad seen Reggie in action. I once tried out for a part in a comedy with a French character and witnessed Reggie in all 'is splendor. 'E is like an onion, with many layers, that man."

"He may break loose when his mother dies."

"Indeed." The tray was set with the precision of a clock maker; the cups and spoons arranged just so. He poured the tea. "Who got the main roles?"

"Do you know Kitty Fairfax? She's the new teacher at the school in Willowbrook who moved in at the beginning of the school year."

"Can't say that I do." He offered Imogen a cup.

"She has a glorious shock of red hair and makes you want to take her home and feed her a good meal."

"Oh! Now I know who you mean. I've seen her walk past the shop a few times."

"Well, she has the most glorious voice. She was quite shy and almost walked off the stage without auditioning, so it was quite unexpected when this incredible sound caressed the room. She's going to play the pirate's fiancée. She'll bring the house down."

"Is that so?" He filled another cup and offered it to Ophelia, her heart skipping as their fingers touched.

Imogen took a sip and realizing she was hungry, reached for one of the cakes. "Des got the role as the pirate. I had no idea he had such stage presence."

One of the ornate clocks marked the hour.

"It does not surprise me. I think as the 'ost of a pub, you must be a bit of a showman."

"That's a great point, Pierre. I hadn't thought of it that way." Ophelia leaned back into the settee. "Another out-of-the-blue performance was Molly Sugden, the new owner of the *Jolly Lolly*. She can sing like a pro and has some stage experience."

"Oh, I know Molly and Ed, 'er 'usband. Very nice people. Molly 'as persuaded Ed to 'elp us with the scenery. Though their boys seem a little rough around the edges."

Imogen quirked a brow. "They're in the play too so that should keep them out of trouble."

"Molly is the fiancée's mother. She'll be fantastic, and Judith the new headmistress is the chaperone. She's a dark horse that one."

"No role for Mildred then?" he said with a wry grin.

"That woman has no ear. She slides off the notes and can't find her way back."

They talked some more about those who had scored main roles in the musical as they finished their tea. Ophelia found herself watching Pierre's hands as he gathered the cups, remembering how deftly those same fingers could pick a lock.

A sudden discordant grinding sound from the elephant clock drew everyone's attention.

Pierre paused, his cup suspended in midair. "*Bizarre!* Everything was working fine yesterday."

He set down the cup and crossed to the clock. Ophelia followed, standing close enough that their shoulders brushed. The elephant's trunk, which should have swayed in its gentle arc, hung motionless.

"The mechanism seems to 'ave stuck," Pierre murmured, more to himself than to them. "I shall 'ave to open it up again."

Imogen stretched and rose from the sofa. "We should head home anyway. Tiger will be pacing the floor."

Ophelia lingered as Imogen headed for the stairs. "Will you be able to fix it?"

"Of course, ma chérie." Pierre's warm smile returned, though his eyes kept darting back to the clock. "It's probably nothing. Just an old spring finally giving way."

But Ophelia had her doubts. Pierre was a master at his work and she had never heard of one of his prized timepieces failing without a cause.

They left him in his workshop, already gathering the special magnifying glasses and other tools of his trade.

Outside, the winter afternoon was drawing to a close, shadows lengthening across the frosted ground. The twins walked arm in arm, their breath forming clouds in the cold air.

"That was odd," said Ophelia.

"What? The clock?" Imogen squeezed her arm. "I agree. I've never heard a clock make quite that sound before. But he's like a clock surgeon. He'll figure it out."

Ophelia nodded but couldn't shake the feeling that the bizarre noise was something more than the mechanism failing.

A low flying duck almost hit them as they passed the pond causing them to let go of each other and jump back with a shriek. All thoughts of the clock departed as Imogen hit the ground with a thud.

Ophelia slid as she grabbed her sister's arm and pulled her up, Imogen rubbing her sore hip. They brushed themselves down, clamped arms again, and chortled the whole way home.

CHAPTER 6

First Rehearsal

"**A**choo!"

"You frightened me to death!" cried Imogen, elbow deep in old costumes.

Since she had volunteered to be the wardrobe manager, she and Ophelia wanted to see what the dramatic society already had. The costume cupboard was actually a room behind the stage.

Ophelia emerged and blew her nose. "It's the dust and moth balls."

There were garments everywhere; some hanging neatly on clothing racks, some thrown on the floor in corners and some in large boxes. They were all in varying stages of decline with some needing to be thrown on the tip while others just needed a good cleaning.

They had brought Tiger who was in doggie heaven with all the new smells. He spent much of the time burrowing under the mounds of clothing.

An arm appeared from the bottom of a pile, holding a dress high and out of the mess. "This might work for the mother."

Imogen waded through outfits spread across the floor and plucked the crumpled gown from her sister's hand.

Holding the dress up, she discovered a shabby, maroon satin garment with a large hoop sewn into the skirt. Some of the lace overlay was in tatters, but those could easily be replaced, and the boned bodice was still intact.

"Well done, lovey! This is perfect."

Tiger jumped like a rabbit in snow, holding something between his enormous jaws.

"What have you got there, big boy?" He dropped the 'gift' at her feet.

It appeared to be a wrinkled tea towel but was in fact, a white shirt that had seen its fair share of performances and never been washed by the smell of it. No wonder it had attracted the dog. She threw it back in the corner for Tiger to chase.

Imogen spotted something green and pulled. A man's wool jacket, in relatively good shape, emerged from the clothing web. It would not fit the rotund Desmond, but it might fit one of Molly's boys. She began a pile of 'hopefuls'.

"Here's another dress," panted Ophelia.

Imogen reached for it and in doing so, spotted some blue trousers. She wrenched them from the confusion, satisfied that with a press, they would be a perfect complement to the green jacket. She draped them over her arm and took hold of the dress. It was a purple, striped, long gown that might work for Kitty if they took it in several inches, or for Celina. She threw them both on her 'hopefuls' pile.

"Here's a corset!" cackled Ophelia. "I'm so glad they're now a thing of the past."

"Throw it to me. The play is set in the last century, so we'll need some of those." She caught the off-white, stained undergarment. The whale bone was still in good shape, in spite of the dirty marks on the fabric. It was a larger size, so it might work for Judith.

After another full hour of hard work, they had divided the costumes on the floor into three piles; rubbish, those in need of mending, and those just needing a wash. Tiger was taking a nap on the pile to be thrown away.

Arms akimbo, Imogen considered their effort. "With regard to mending and washing, I think I'll ask the Women's Institute to help. It's too big a job for two people."

"Splendid idea." Ophelia wiped her nose again.

"Let's get started on the costumes hanging on the rack. It looks like they're in better shape."

By the end of another twenty minutes, they had sorted costumes for several of the women in the chorus, some of the pirates, the fiancée's mother and the chaperone. Nothing suitable had been unearthed for the admiral or the pirate Leopold, 'Lucky', Blackwood; they would need to make their costumes from scratch. Plus, the wedding gown for the leading lady.

"What are you going to do after you get these existing costumes mended and washed. If they end up on the floor again, they'll get ruined and all our hard work will be for naught."

"Let's see if Pierre or Des can construct some more clothing racks. Three more should do it; one for female costumes, one for males' and one for the children's."

They exited the cupboard and ran straight into the caretaker, Rex Stout, whose head snapped back with surprise. Readjusting his hat, he gasped, "What on earth?"

"We've been sorting out the costumes," Imogen explained as Rex rested his chin on the broom he was holding. Tiger sniffed his shoes.

"Well, you look a right sight," he chuckled, keeping one eye on the enormous dog.

The twins examined each other. They were covered in dust and bits of fabric and thread, and Ophelia's hair looked like that of a scarecrow.

"What a fright we look! I was going to suggest going to *Thyme For Tea* to get a drink and give Matilda the good news, but I think we need to go home and tidy up first.

"Can I have everyone's attention, please?" cried Matilda over the hubbub. "Collin! What did I tell you about the curtains. Do you want me to have your mother come to the practice?"

Collin slid down the drapes pronto.

"Right! Let's run through the ladies' chorus followed by the pirates' chorus in Act I, scene I. All chorus actors on stage, please.

Clomp, clomp. The crowd of actors jostled into position. Matilda rearranged them by height.

"Men and boys, you will stand watching the ladies sing as if you find them extremely interesting."

"If we were real pirates who'd just returned from months at sea, we would find the ladies more than interesting," chortled Des.

"Exactly." Matilda turned, almost falling off the edge of the stage. "Whoops! That would've been nasty." She ran a hand over her chest. "Ophelia, ladies' chorus, please."

Ophelia started to play, but the ladies came in weakly, clearly unsure of their lines.

"Let's get some scripts up here," shouted Matilda, her hair falling down around her ears. Prudence Creswell, the vicar's wife, ran the scripts to the stage and handed them out.

"Again, from the top!" commanded Matilda.

Music in hand, the ladies sang out enthusiastically, but Collin and Tommy began to fight with invisible swords behind them.

"Tommy! Stop that at once! Remember, you're on stage to watch the ladies as if they are the most interesting creatures you have ever seen." Collin and Tommy mimed throwing up.

"Ladies, keep singing," she shouted waving her arms up and down.

For a first attempt, it wasn't too bad and Mildred was able to stay on tune by following the other ladies in the chorus.

Matilda gestured with her arm. "Right. Ladies, move to the edges and cluster on each side of the men. It is your turn to watch the men sing with an expression of mild curiosity. Men move forward. And go!"

The men were nothing short of awful. They did not know their words or the tune, and it was painful to listen. "Tomorrow, practice with the men's chorus only to learn the songs. We don't have time for that today. Tomorrow at seven sharp. Got that Collin?"

"Yes, ma'am." He saluted.

"Miss Rutherford. Are you here?" Matilda put a hand to her forehead and looked out into the hall.

The headmistress stepped forward. "Here I am, Matilda."

"Good. Let's teach the men their dance."

For the next half an hour, the twins stifled laughter as Judith attempted to teach the men the sailor's hornpipe. The only male who was any good, was David, one of Molly's boys.

"It will come, it will come," cried Matilda, examining her clipboard. "Practice it at home, please. Ladies, it's your turn."

Judith ran them through a Regency-type dance. This time everyone picked it up remarkably quickly, except Mildred who kept turning the wrong way. At this rate, the dancing would bring the house down in a way it was not supposed to.

After twenty minutes, Matilda cut them off. "Thank you, ladies. Again, practice at home, please. Right, men's and women's choruses, you may go home. Next practice for everyone is Friday at seven. Pirates, I'll see you tomorrow."

The crowd of young actors fell, jumped or were pushed off the stage while the older set took the stairs.

The noise level in the hall fell considerably and Matilda expelled a sigh of relief.

"It's always challenging at the very beginning," she assured the twins. "That's what practices are for." She gathered up her hair and stuck some pins in it. "Soloists!"

Celina, Judith, Molly, Des and Farmer Jones appeared on the stage.

Matilda looked harried. "Where's Kitty?"

"She was here a minute ago," replied Celina, looking around the hall.

"Someone find her!" ordered Matilda.

"I'll go," offered Imogen, who thought perhaps Kitty was in the ladies' room.

Not finding her there, she looked in the costume cupboard, the kitchen and then outside in the blistering cold. A northeast wind had picked up that afternoon and as the sun had set, temperatures dropped below freezing. Imogen wrapped her coat tightly around her, pulling the hat low over her ears.

"Kitty! Kitty, dear! You're on!" The gale whipped Imogen's voice away.

Not finding the young teacher outside the front of the hall, Imogen followed the side of the building to the back where it was almost pitch black. Two figures appeared clumped together.

"Kitty?"

One of the figures fled with a lumbering gait and Kitty looked up with fear in her eyes.

"Who was that?" asked Imogen trying to make out the young woman's face in the dark.

"No one. You must have seen a shadow made by the moon, Mrs. Pettigrew. I'm—I'm here alone. I j-just needed some air."

Why lie? Imogen let the matter drop.

"Well, you're going to catch your death out here without a hat. Come on inside. You're up."

Kitty followed in her wake and when Imogen saw her in the electric light, it was evident that all was not well. Her creamy skin was pale as milk and her eyes had a wild look.

"Are you sure you're alright?" asked Imogen.

"Never better." Kitty almost ran onto the stage.

Curious about the girl's deception, Imogen grabbed her torch and went back outside to the place she had found Kitty with the man. Why had the girl not told the truth? It was dark, but Imogen knew the difference between a shadow and a human being.

The gusts had picked up into a real gale, and she held onto her hat as the branches moaned and the owls hooted. She took the torch from her pocket and swung the beam around. Next to a broad tree trunk, sat a small pile of cigarettes. She put on a glove, picked up one of the used cigarette ends and held it to her nose. Drawing back at the sharp tang of the cheaper brands of cigarettes, she wrinkled her nose in distaste. She had not smelled smoke on Kitty at any time and her tiny home had not held the odor. She put the used-up cigarette in her pocket.

Swinging the beam around again, she found half a bus ticket flapping in the breeze. The bus conductor had torn the ticket in half so that it could not be used again but she could still make out that it was from Parkford to Saffron Weald from that afternoon. There would be no more buses back to Parkford until tomorrow morning. She popped it in her pocket and returned to the hall.

The rest of the practice went well, though Kitty was not nearly as charismatic as she had been in the audition. Imogen noticed her hands were not too steady and that she missed a couple of cues. Matilda could not hide her disappointment. At one point, Imogen caught Kitty's eye, but she quickly looked away.

At nine o'clock, Matilda called an end to the practice. Kitty bolted before anyone else had even got their coats on and Imogen heard fragments of conversation from the other actors about Kitty's poor performance.

Celina and Judith left together, Judith poking her finger into a small hole in her canvas bag, explaining it was a gift from a friend.

"Something has certainly unsettled Miss Fairfax," complained Matilda as she shrugged into her coat and made for the door. "I do hope she can pull it together or I shall have to swap her with Celina."

Imogen put a hand on her sister's arm to indicate that they should wait a moment. Ophelia frowned. Rex Stout began sweeping the empty hall.

Once Imogen was sure Matilda was out of sight, she led Ophelia to the door and they stepped out into the stormy night.

"Someone was outside with Kitty when I found her."

Ophelia stopped in her tracks. "What? Who?"

"I don't know. I couldn't see in the dark, but I'd wager by the size and shape, it was a man."

"Is that all?" huffed Ophelia. "A sweetheart?"

"No, no. You've got it all wrong, lovey. You didn't see Kitty's face—like she'd seen a ghost."

Ophelia pulled up her coat collar as the biting cold tempest blasted her face. "She did seem rather off tonight."

"Kitty was terrified. Whoever it was, scared her and she couldn't pull herself together to perform."

An owl screeched.

"Didn't you ask her who it was?"

"Of course! She denied anyone was there. She practically told me I'd imagined it, but I *know* what I saw."

Ophelia looked up at the branches swaying and groaning. "In this weather you may have been mistaken."

"But—"

Imogen stopped short as a chill swept over her. She looked behind them, peering into the darkness.

"What is it?"

"I think someone is following us."

A switch flipped in Ophelia. She pulled Imogen behind a tree, scanning the churchyard with eyes that seemed to see in the dark.

Ophelia raised a hand.

Imogen's heart jumped into her throat.

Nothing.

Ophelia continued to peer into the inky blackness like the bird of prey above them as Imogen felt fear slice through her.

In a hoarse whisper, Ophelia asked, "Why are you so certain Kitty lied to you?"

"Because I found some warm cigarette ends and a bus ticket to Saffron Weald from Parkford from this afternoon."

"Bravo, ducky. You were right, but whoever it was, has gone now."

"How do you know?"

"I saw a slight shadow and a depression in the grass, but when they saw me watching, they slunk away into the churchyard."

"I wish we had Tiger with us. He would find them and pin them to the ground. Let's get home before—"

"Before what?" Ophelia's tone was sharp. "If anyone tries anything, they'll rue the day they messed with us."

The wind howled through the trees behind them. Imogen gripped her sister's arm as they hurried home, wondering if Kitty's terror would soon become their own.

CHAPTER 7

Satin and Secrets

T he sounds of chatter and comfortable laughter filled the village hall amid the whir and pump of treadle sewing machines and the snap of fabric scissors. An organized chaos of swatches bought with the last play's ticket revenues, dominated the trestle tables – midnight blue velvet that caught the light with each movement, delicate ivory satin that whispered with every touch, and yards of wine-colored taffeta that rustled like autumn leaves. The leading lady's ball gown sprawled across three chairs, its beadwork catching the afternoon sun, while a couple of partially finished chorus costumes threatened to topple over the end of the table.

Harriet Cleaver, the butcher, sat surrounded by a cloud of the cream-colored satin, carefully piecing together the fiancée's wedding dress for the final scene, while Molly Sugden muttered under her breath as she wrestled with the stiff brocade of the admiral's coat. Ribbons, buttons, and scraps of lace were scattered like confetti across every surface, casualties of the WI's emergency costume brigade.

Mildred Chumbley might be a critical, carping gossip, but even her harshest critics could not deny her talent for marshaling the WI's forces in a crisis.

Alice Puddingfield arrived with a tray of delicacies from the bakery and the whole crowd cheered. She placed the tray in the middle of the mess of notions and scattered teacups and took a seat next to Ophelia.

Removing her hat, Alice swept a floury hand over her blonde-gray hair. "I couldn't get away any sooner. We got an order for fairy cakes for a wedding and Archie needed me."

Imogen shook her head. "You don't have to make excuses, Alice. We know bakers are always busy. I'm just glad you made it."

"Tell me what to do before the chief bosses me around." Alice cast a wary eye at the top of the table where Mildred sat like a general surveying her troops.

"Can you sew by hand?" asked Imogen.

"I darn socks and mend tears."

"Perfect." Imogen pulled a dress from a pile and showed Alice two rips in the skirt and a spot where the hem had come undone. "You can start with this."

The door opened again letting in a blast of cold winter air.

"Kitty! Here for your fitting?" asked Mildred, before Imogen could get a word in.

"Yes, I just got back from school." The fiery mane that poked out from under her hat was tangled and windswept from her long bike ride, her cheeks chapped red.

"Patricia. Are you sewing the fiancée's day dress?" asked Mildred.

Patricia nodded, her mouth full of pins.

"Imogen, can you help size Kitty's dress with Patricia?"

Although Imogen was technically in charge of matters concerning the costumes, she allowed Mildred to take the lead as it was she who had rallied the troops. "Of course."

When Kitty shrugged off her coat, the contrast between her practical school clothes and the elaborate costume awaiting her on Patricia's lap could not have been starker. Patricia had crafted a romantic heroine's dress from iridescent silk taffeta that shifted from deep purple to midnight blue, its fitted bodice scattered with tiny crystal beads that winked like stars.

"Arms up," Imogen instructed, holding the partially pinned costume ready. Shooting her arms into the air, a slight moan escaped Kitty's lips. As Imogen slipped the half-finished gown over her head, the young teacher's excitement was palpable, her usual sunny disposition even brighter. The silk rustled against Kitty's wool skirt as Patricia began pinning and adjusting.

"I've never worn anything this beautiful," Kitty gasped.

Across the room, Harriet looked up from the incomplete wedding dress, its cream satin and delicate lace spilling across her lap. "It's all in the details, dear. The pearly buttons on *this* gown will make it extra special."

The young schoolteacher turned to try to catch another glimpse of the wedding gown. "Will it have sleeves like this one?"

"Kitty, do stay still," pleaded Patricia, "or I'll never get these alterations marked properly."

"I was going to make short, puffed sleeves with little bows," answered Harriet.

"Would you mind terribly making it with sleeves," Kitty begged. "I just hate my skinny arms."

"Since I haven't got to that part yet, I daresay I can add a long sleeve, if you wish." Harriet gave her a smile.

"Thank you, Mrs. Cleaver. It's so beautiful."

The young woman's bright mood indicated that she had recovered from the mental distress caused by the mysterious stranger during the first rehearsal, and Imogen was not about to pry and ruin her good humor. Besides, Kitty had made it clear the subject was closed.

"Did you hear that Pierre is missing a valuable ring?" said Harriet to Celina.

Even with the cheerful hubbub, Imogen came to an abrupt standstill at the snippet of conversation.

"I don't mean to eavesdrop, but did you say Pierre has had something stolen?"

Though she had not heard the original comment, Ophelia did

hear her sister through the noise and looked up with concern.

"Yes, I was passing his shop this morning on the way to *Tumblethorn's,* and I bumped into Constable Hargrove." Harriet looked at Imogen with earnest eyes.

Everyone quieted their own conversations to listen.

"Do you know any of the details?" asked Ophelia.

"No, just that the ring is gone."

Placing the needle work on the table, Ophelia asked, "And nothing else was missing?"

"Not as far as I know."

Ophelia's expression transformed from concern to distress.

"Go!" said Imogen. "There are plenty of us to get this done."

Ophelia grabbed her coat, still pulling it on as she headed through the door into the winter landscape.

She and Pierre had renewed their friendship since her return to Saffron Weald and things were progressing to the point that she thought he might propose. Neither one of them had ever been married; he because the love of his youth had died, and she because she had chosen the violin and independence.

She flew through the antique shop's door, nearly knocking the little bell off its hook. Pierre was alone and she threw herself into his arms.

"I just heard."

He pulled her gently back so he could look into her face. "About the ring?"

Brushing his hand across her forehead, she shivered. "Yes. The ring."

Gesturing with his arm, while holding her close with the other, he soothed her. "It is not too tragic, chérie, though it *was* quite valuable. It once belonged to the Duchess of Kent." Pierre's eyes gleamed as they always did when discussing historical treasures. "The story goes that she commissioned it in 1805 as a memorial piece after the death of her 'usband. It 'ad a distinctive setting – three small sapphires representing 'er children, surrounding a central diamond. The ring passed through several 'ands before ending up in a private collection in Devon. I acquired it just last month from an estate sale." He paused, frowning slightly. "What I cannot understand is why they stole just the one. Why not grab them all? It would have been easily done."

"Perhaps the thief was interrupted."

"Could be, but they were all nestled together in a little display dish."

"Let's just be grateful." She leaned her head against his. "Nonetheless, your shop *has* been violated."

"That is true, but they could 'ave taken a lot more. I think I need to 'am up my security."

She giggled. "*Beef* up your security."

"Yes. That's it."

She switched into sleuth mode. "Show me where it was."

He led her to the left side of his shop. All the merchandise was artfully displayed and he pointed to a piece of black velvet swirled in a dish upon which sat several antique rings.

"When did you notice it was missing?"

"This morning, while I was dusting, but I confess, it could 'ave been gone for a week since that is the last time I dusted."

Only someone searching for the ring would have noticed its absence among the others, like a missing star in a familiar constellation.

She touched his arm. "Have you had any customers you didn't know over the last week?"

"Well, that's the thing. I 'ad a group of elderly visitors who were on a rambling 'oliday and stopped in on a recommendation by the tour guide. Then there was the Meadowshire Birdwatchers Association who were in Saffron Weald after a sighting of a rare thrush. It's actually been quite a busy week."

"So, what you are saying is, anyone could have taken it."

He sighed. "Yes. I 'ave become less suspicious in my old age; more trusting of people."

"Sounds like you need to dust off some old skills." They shared an understanding. "How will the police ever find it?"

"I have already spoken to them. They will send a description to all the pawn brokers and antique dealers in this county and those that surround it. But I fear it is lost … which is a shame."

Something in his tone made her catch his eye. He winked. "I 'ad designs on that particular ring."

Ophelia caught her breath.

"But all is well. I shall just search for another worthy jewel." He kissed her and all thoughts of the missing ring disappeared.

He turned the sign on the door to 'closed'. "Would you like some tea?"

"I've just had my fill at the village hall. We're fixing up the old costumes and creating new ones under the stern leadership of Mildred."

"I thought Matilda 'ad put your sister in charge of the costumes?"

"She did, but you know Mildred."

"Well, let me offer you some entertainment then. I just got a new record."

"That sounds delightful." She followed him up the stairs to his home and looked around the room. The automaton clock was still missing from the sideboard.

"Have you not mended the elephant clock?"

"As it 'appens, I am in the middle of taking it apart. I've been busy with the scenery for the play." He gestured to his desk which held some of the tools from his workshop and the disemboweled clock. "I'm still not sure what is wrong."

"Can I watch you work while we listen to the gramophone?"

"Won't you find it tiresome?"

She smiled. "Nothing you do is tiresome."

He produced that sultry grin that set her heart thumping. "If you insist."

Laying the record on the turntable, he set the needle. The full rich sounds of the symphony filled the room and Ophelia drank it in. Taking her hand, he led her to the desk and dragged a chair across the room for her to sit on. Switching on the special light, he placed the magnifying glasses on his nose.

Several tiny cogs lay on a mat and the back of the clock was off showing the inner workings of the beautiful piece. Pierre set to work with tweezers gently moving more of the delicate wires.

"I cannot understand it. There seems to be no reason … wait, what is this?"

He raised the tweezers high and Ophelia saw a small key clutched in its jaws. He dropped it into her hand. The filigree bow grip of the key was strikingly delicate, almost like a piece of jewelry.

"What on earth …?" But even as she said it, she thought of the key to her own treasure box hidden under the bed in London. "Could it be to a personal document box?"

Pierre grinned as her deductive reasoning skills were set in motion by the puzzle. "More importantly, what was it doing in my clock!"

"Has the clock been up here since you purchased it?"

His eyes rolled up as he considered her question. "No. I displayed it on the floor for a while but I 'ad a sign on it that said, 'not for sale'."

"Someone has been staking out your store, it would seem. I agree that you need to increase your security measures."

"What security measures?" he chuckled. "But seriously, I've already called the Parkford locksmith to replace the old lock on the front door with a Chubb."

Ophelia was in no mood for humor. "What about the back? Anyone could hang about in the alley and slip in unnoticed after hours."

"You're right. I'll 'ave 'im change that one too. But it's a shame when you 'ave to do that in sleepy Saffron Weald."

She twisted her lips. "Do I need to remind you that we have had several murders over the last few months?"

He tapped her nose. "It 'as not escaped my notice that they 'ave occurred since your return, my dear."

She could not deny it.

He reached for a drawer on his desk and pulled out a fine gold chain. "Since the integrity of my shop 'as been compromised, I think it a good idea for you to keep this safe for me." He slipped the small key onto the chain and hung it around her neck, the tickling sensation causing her pulse to become erratic. She placed her finger on the key then slipped it under her sweater.

"Will you tell Constable Hargrove about this?"

"Since it was *added* to my store and not stolen, I think I will keep it to myself for a while. We don't want whoever put it there to be alerted to the fact that we 'ave discovered it."

She snapped her fingers. "We could use the clock to set a trap."

He caught on to her meaning immediately. "I shall put it all together again and return it to the display shelf while I surveille every customer who comes in."

Ophelia studied the spot where the small key had rested hidden in the clock's mechanism. Someone had gone to considerable trouble to conceal it there. As Pierre began reassembling the delicate gears, she touched the chain around her neck where the key now hung. Whatever secret it unlocked, someone would eventually come looking for it, and when they did, Ophelia and Pierre would be ready.

CHAPTER 8

Dress Rehearsal

The backstage area of the village hall had transformed into a war zone of costumes, props, and frayed nerves. Someone had spilled coffee on Imogen's prompt script, the admiral's magnificent brocade coat was missing a crucial button, and Mildred Chumbley was holding court in the wings, announcing each technical mishap with the grim satisfaction of a prophet whose dire predictions had finally come true.

Amateur dramatics, Imogen was learning, was rather like juggling eggs while riding a bicycle; possible, but with a high likelihood of making a mess.

"Get down, Collin!" cried Imogen. "I thought we made it clear there was to be no climbing the curtains."

Shocked by her cry, he lost his grip and fell to the floor with a bang.

Her heart stopped. "Anything broken?"

Collin wiggled both ankles. "Nope."

"Well, hopefully you've learned your lesson," she said, as he limped into the wings holding his backside.

"Where is my fiancée?" shouted Matilda.

"She's never said that before", thought Ophelia uncharitably, from her seat at the piano. She had spent the last few weeks

practicing the songs with the actors to make sure they knew all the words.

"Where *is* my fiancée?" repeated Matilda.

A tiny hand shot up from the third row. "I'm here."

"Come to the front dear, where I can see you."

Kitty's wild hair had been wrestled into a beautiful bun with curls framing her face. The exotic gown created by Harriet gave the illusion of curves and somehow made Kitty look taller and less waif-like. Her green eyes popped behind the stage makeup. More than one male jaw dropped as she emerged onto the front of the stage.

"Oh, my dear! What a transformation!" gasped Matilda.

Kitty dipped her head with pleasurable embarrassment.

"Right! Des. Move over here." Matilda's ears were scarlet as she tried to bring some semblance of order to the madness.

Des stepped forward, marvelous in striped pirate trousers and blousy, white shirt with a colorful fabric belt. A matching scarf around his head and a hooped earring completed the outfit.

"Molly and Judith."

Molly Sugden had also been transformed. The gown with the hooped skirt and rips had been repaired, fitted and cleaned and looked brand new. She wore a Marie Antoinette wig that rose high from her head and a large beauty spot had been penciled onto rouged cheeks.

This was the fun of the theater; you could become a different person with every new play.

As the chaperone, Judith's metamorphosis was less dramatic, but her long gown of dove gray muslin was still flattering.

"Who am I missing?" murmured Matilda.

"Me," said Celina, pushing between the men of the pirate's chorus. As the particular friend of the fiancée, her blood red gown was of equal splendor. Celina was pretty by any standard but the curve of her neck, revealed by the upsweep of her black hair, and the contrast of her blue eyes to the black kohl, unwittingly upstaged Kitty.

"Lovely, Celina. Stand here next to Kitty, please."

Matilda checked her list. "Where is Farmer Jones."

"He's just dressing," said Reggie. "It's planting season and he had to get it finished today before the rain forecast for tomorrow."

"Hmm, well, he doesn't appear till the end of the first act so we can get started. Everyone who is not in the opening scene, please secrete yourselves in the wings."

Prudence Cresswell and Imogen, acting as stage managers, were responsible for all the props and making sure the actors got on and off stage in time. The opening scene was a stroll on the prom at a coastal watering hole. The backdrop created by Reggie showed the beach and sea with white caps. The only prop needed was an iron railing that represented the prom. The pirate's chorus dragged it into the middle of the stage.

Turning, Matilda gestured to Ophelia to play the opening bars.

"Go, go, go!" commanded Imogen, gently pushing the four women forward.

As soon as Kitty began to sing, the rest of the cast stopped talking. Her voice was pure magic.

Halfway through the first number, Farmer Jones struggled into the wings. Someone had sewn the button back on his coat and except for the brightness on his cheeks, he looked every inch the naval admiral.

"Just in time," whispered Imogen, nudging him onto the stage.

Except for a couple of forgotten lines, the first scene went off without a hitch.

Ophelia played the intro to the pirate's hornpipe for scene two, but the men were still dragging off the promenade railing.

"Hold it!" shouted Matilda. "We still have to get the ship prop on." She turned to Ophelia. "Can you play a refrain of the fiancée's solo to give them time to change the scenery?"

Pierre and Ed Sugden had fitted the ship with wheels for easy movement, but it still took a couple of minutes to situate it properly on the stage, and the extra music gave them time to replace the scenery and position themselves for the pirate's dance.

Judith had choreographed all the numbers and after private discussion with Matilda they had agreed to let Reggie's personal flair shine through. As Reggie twirled with abandon, center stage, dressed in scarlet and green striped pirate trousers, the rest of the boys and Des performed a traditional hornpipe. The whole aging stage seemed to become part of the performance, contributing its own soundtrack of squeaks, groans, and whispers.

Reggie possessed a sunny disposition by nature, but tonight his joy seemed to spill from him like light, transforming the tired village hall into something magical.

Des missed his line, but Prudence prompted him from the other side of the stage, and one of the Sugden boys' trousers fell down around his ankles but Imogen quickly ran on with a safety pin to preserve his dignity.

Without being asked, Ophelia played a refrain again to give the men time to swap out the scenery.

"Where's the table?" cried Matilda as the ship was wheeled off. "We need the table and chairs for the dining room scene."

Imogen checked her notes. "Collin and Tommy. You need to grab the table as soon as you exit the stage."

Matilda waved her arms wildly. "And we've got the wrong back drop."

Oops. Imogen rushed to the rope pulley, lifting the ocean scene and revealing the indoor Victorian dining room.

The women from the ladies' chorus each grabbed a chair, placing them around the table as the main characters took their positions.

Backstage, the turmoil continued its own frenzied dance: the rustle of taffeta and satin as actresses squeezed past each other in the narrow spaces, and the hollow clatter of various props being arranged and rearranged. Above it all, dust motes swirled in the air, caught in the stark beams of light that leaked through gaps in the upper curtains.

"I need the blue lights," said Matilda.

That was a problem. "I don't have time to do the lights *and* switch the backdrop," yelled Imogen. "We'll need to assign someone else to do the lights."

"I can 'elp." Pierre had just arrived to watch the dress rehearsal.

Ophelia's eyes followed him as he hurried across the hall and arrived at Imogen's side in the wings, positioning himself by the stage lights.

"Let's try that scene change again. Bring back the ship, take off the table and carry it back on. We need that to be a smoother transition. That is what dress rehearsals are all about."

There was a burst of grumbling headed by Mildred.

"Must we replace the backdrop again?" The pulley was old and in need of oiling. It took all of Imogen's strength to shift it, and her muscles were burning.

"No. Just the props."

"Would you prefer me to do the backdrop?" Pierre asked Imogen. "I know 'ow 'eavy they are because we 'ad to 'ang them all yesterday."

Though she was tempted by his suggestion, it was not practical. "I appreciate the offer but unfortunately, I'm better positioned to do that than the lights. A little bit of oil will go a long way." She made a mental note to bring oil before the performance.

"Let's try it again," shouted Matilda.

Ophelia played the refrain and the younger boys galloped off and returned, carrying the table as the older boys and Des wheeled off the ship.

"Much better. Main ladies, as soon as Ophelia changes the music to the intro to the next scene, find your seat at the table."

"We don't have any plates or glasses," said Celina.

"My mistake," admitted Pru, her hair awry, stepping onto the stage with her prompt manuscript. "I'll see to it."

"I should have been in charge of props instead of having this insignificant part," grumbled Mildred, loud enough for everyone to hear. "I wouldn't have forgotten anything."

Pru's face fell as she directed the ladies' chorus to the box with the dinnerware. They raced out with the plates and wine glasses. "Are they supposed to have anything in them?" asked Alice, wiping drops from her gown.

Matilda waved her hand. "No. But never mind that for now. And, action!"

The ladies' chorus members hurried off as the scene began.

Apart from a wig that slipped and a broken shoe strap, the scene ran smoothly and Imogen pulled the rope in the opposite direction to replace the dining room with the ocean backdrop.

In the next scene, the widow Prudentia Bottomley-Blythe was to cross paths with the admiral who is immediately captivated and decides to court her.

"Farmer Jones!" called Imogen. "You're needed on stage again."

He materialized from the shadows of the wings, face flushed and glistening with sweat. The admiral's brocade coat, though magnificent, was clearly stifling after a long day spent in the fields. Imogen noticed how he kept tugging at the high collar, his weathered face unusually red.

Wiping his mouth, he apologized for being tardy. "Sorry, I was so thirsty. I've been out on the land all day."

Imogen shooed him toward the stage where he stepped into the bright lights, attempting to slow his pace to his character's genteel stroll along the promenade.

The small group of ladies approached right on cue, but their expressions turned to alarm on setting eyes on the farmer. As he attempted his courtly stroll, his usual confident stride faltered and he seemed to squint against the stage lights as if they pained him. When he raised his hand to doff his hat, the gesture was unsteady. He opened his mouth to sing, but instead, his face contorted in confusion and pain.

"Something's wrong," Pierre whispered to Imogen from his position by the light panel. Several chorus members shifted uneasily.

Prudence peeked out from the curtains. "Farmer Jones? Are

you quite well?"

Jones attempted to sing again but only managed to produce a choked gurgling sound before clutching his throat and stumbling sideways. His expression of bewilderment evolved into dawning panic. The admiral's hat slipped from his trembling fingers, landing with a soft thud on the boards. Then to everyone's horror, his knees buckled, and Farmer Jones crashed to the stage with a thud that was far too real for any performance.

Imogen froze. *This could* not *be happening again!*

"Farmer Jones! Farmer Jones! What are you doing? There is no death scene," cried Matilda losing her patience. "Get up, man." Her voice shifted from irritation to concern when she saw how he jerked on the floor, his face turning an alarming shade of purple.

The music stuttered to a halt as Ophelia's hands froze on the piano keys.

Celina's blood-red gown blazed across the stage as she dashed over to assist him. "Help! He's choking!" Her dress swirled around her knees as she knelt by the farmer writhing on the floor.

The spell of shock shattered and Imogen and Pierre burst onto the stage. Pierre cradled the farmer's head while pounding his back, but the farmer's convulsions were already weakening. His eyes, wide with panic and confusion, darted around the faces above him before rolling back in his head. One final, violent spasm shook his body, before he went terrifyingly limp.

The silence that followed was absolute. Even the old building seemed to hold its breath as Imogen reached trembling fingers toward his neck. She had to try twice before she could steady her hand enough to check for a pulse. The skin beneath her touch was already cooling.

"*Hot crumpets!*" she whispered, her face draining of color. "He's dead!"

CHAPTER 9

Exit Stage Right

Imogen's stark words hovered in the air before bedlam erupted. Matilda fainted dead away, caught just in time by Desmond, who leapt off the stage. The chorus members stumbled backward, costumes rustling. Ironically, Mildred was stunned into silence.

Ophelia abandoned her piano, but Imogen's firm voice cut through the pandemonium.

"Stay in the hall! Nobody leave!" She called to the vicar's wife. "Pru, can you pop to the vicarage and call Parkford for the doctor. Tommy, go and fetch Constable Hargrove and come right back. Do you understand?"

Tommy nodded noiselessly and slipped out the door as Matilda came around and Des led her to a chair.

Ophelia looked up to see Kitty, frozen center stage, one hand pressed to her mouth, eyes fixed on the body while Molly gripped her other arm as if to steady them both. The makeup Kitty had carefully applied was smudged with tears.

Reggie began to pace on the spot, hands trembling.

Seeing the symptoms of shock in those around her, Imogen made a decision.

"Mildred, are the tea supplies for WI meetings in the

cupboard?"

Mildred's shock began to ebb. "Yes. That's what we all need; sweet tea." She made for the kitchen.

Imogen turned back to the stage. "Come down and sit on the chairs. We'll get you something to drink."

Now that the alarmed chatter had subsided, they all obeyed as if in a trance.

"I'll help Mildred," offered Alice.

"And I'll cover up the body and stop people going backstage," said Pierre.

"Thank you."

Ophelia began leading people to the chairs set up in the room.

"What are you thinking?" she asked her sister softly.

"I hope it was natural causes—"

"—but?"

"Look at his skin. It's too pink."

"You think it was … " Ophelia dropped her voice further so no one else would hear. "Cyanide?" She wondered how her widowed sister knew the symptoms of cyanide poisoning.

"Together with the stumbling and convulsions, plus when I felt his pulse there was the distinct smell of vomit."

"Well, as far as anyone else knows, Farmer Jones died from a heart attack or stroke so I think it best to let them think that until the authorities get here."

"Agreed. Pierre has gone to keep people from going backstage. I believe he saw the signs of cyanide poisoning too."

At that moment the door banged open revealing Constable Hargrove and Tommy looking white as a sheet. Everyone was on edge and jumped at the noise.

Ophelia pointed to the shrouded body.

"Would you say we are looking at a horrible health incident?" asked the constable, his usually slack face strained with concern, his chin worrying the strap of his helmet.

Imogen pursed her lips. "Well … I'll let you be the judge of that. We've called Dr. Pemberton."

"Right." The biblical phrase, 'girding one's loins', came to mind as the policeman approached the stage.

"If it is poison, we should take a quick look at everything backstage," said Ophelia. "Why don't you aid the constable while I take a gander?"

"Good idea."

They both mounted the stairs and Imogen approached Constable Hargrove. "What do you think of the color of his skin?"

The constable's brow furrowed.

"Aren't the deceased usually rather gray?" she prompted as Ophelia slunk off to go backstage.

Ophelia thought back to just before Farmer Jones' entrance. He had come from stage right, where the dining table had been moved. A memory flashed – Alice wiping her dress where liquid had spilled from one of the prop glasses. But that made no sense. While the glasses would contain water during the actual performance for authenticity, they were supposed to be empty during rehearsal.

Upon reaching the wings, Ophelia saw Pierre standing guard backstage. He raised an arm in understanding of her purpose.

Locating the prop dining table, she was pleased to see the glasses still there. She examined each one using a handkerchief she had in her pocket. There were four glasses in total, but the third one had a trace of liquid in the bottom. She sniffed. *Bitter almond.* The solution to the farmer's demise burst upon her senses. Seized by thirst before his important solo, he had seen the water and grabbed the glass to wet his whistle, sealing his fate.

A second realization hit. The farmer's drinking from the glass was a completely random act that could not have been anticipated. *Someone had put poison in the glass to kill one of the ladies at the table.*

She wrapped the wineglass in the handkerchief and hurried across the stage telegraphing to her sister that she had made a discovery of great significance.

"Constable Hargrove. I've found something you will want to

see." She offered him the wrapped glass.

Having become accustomed to assistance from the quick-witted twins, he merely shrugged and took the empty glass with a query on his brow.

"Take a sniff," Ophelia suggested.

Obeying, he caught her eye, still confused.

"Can you not smell it?" She remembered from her past being informed that some people could not smell the presence of cyanide.

"Smell what?"

Ophelia made sure no one else was listening. "It's cyanide."

The constable started before his face collapsed with regret. "You're telling me we have *another* murder on our hands?"

"I'm afraid so," Ophelia responded. "Time to call the inspector, I think. Shall I have the vicar's wife do that? They have a telephone in the vicarage."

Constable Hargrove nodded.

"That would also explain the pink hue of his skin," added Imogen.

Staring at the glass he asked, "Who on earth would want to kill Nicholas Jones?"

Ophelia lowered her voice to a hoarse whisper. "It gets even worse, Constable. I do not believe Farmer Jones was the intended target. He merely took a drink of what he thought was water before going onstage to sing his solo. The glasses had just been used in the scene before, a scene in which the four leading ladies sat at a dinner table." She waited for her news to sink in.

Imogen grabbed her arm with fiery eyes.

The constable's head swung around like an owl searching for prey. "You mean one of those four ladies was the intended target?"

"Yes! That's exactly what I'm suggesting." She tipped her head to indicate to Imogen to search the area for further clues.

The constable's face paled at the implication. "Who *are* the leading ladies?" He removed his notebook to record the names Ophelia gave him. "Do you know who was sitting by that particular glass?"

This was a problem Ophelia had considered ever since her discovery a few moments before; unless the murderer was Alice, who they knew had placed the filled glass on the table, the killer had been catastrophically sloppy. In the mayhem of the rehearsal, it was impossible to guarantee that the intended victim would be the one to get the poisoned glass. Furthermore, if the table had been rotated at all during removal, the original position of the glasses would have been compromised.

Slipping away to the wings, Imogen studied everything on the right side of the stage. It was a complete shambles of furniture, large pieces of scenery, discarded costumes and small props. She sighed with frustration. Everything could be a potential clue. And nothing.

She got down on all fours.

The floor was strewn with debris - feathers, loose threads, a stubbed out cigarette and sewing pins; but was any of it relevant?

Crawling around under the table and behind the facade of the ship, she discovered a tiny mother of pearl button, a torn shred of telegram, a flattened thimble, a link from a housekeeper's chatelaine and a fraction of a pawn ticket. Carefully gathering them into her pocket she had little hope they would be of value, given the caretaker's casual approach to cleaning. Frankly, they could have been lying there for decades.

As she crossed the stage she noticed Pierre behind the backdrop.

"Did you find anything?" he asked. "I saw you looking for clues. Is it confirmed that this was a murder?"

For an expert in antiques, he was rather familiar with investigation techniques.

Joining him, she spoke in a low tone. "We found dregs of cyanide in one of the prop wineglasses—"

"—but that means the murderer was targeting one of the ladies."

He seemed to have fathomed the whole sordid crime in a

moment.

"Yes. Ophelia just gave the constable the bad news and sent me to search for clues before everything is disturbed by well-meaning policemen.

"Good luck finding anything of worth in this clutter."

"Exactly. Ophelia and I acted on this stage in our youth and I doubt the custodians over the years have been too particular."

"Well, I can report that no one has come back here since the murder."

"That's something, I suppose." She gave him a little smile and continued on to the other side of the stage.

Chairs and scattered parasols lay next to shoes and a clothing rack for quick changes. A needle winked at her in the backstage lights. It was the definition of a needle in a haystack. Once again, she dropped to her knees and scoured the floor.

This time she found a trodden down book of matches from the *Lion Hotel* in Parkford, a seamstress's measuring tape, an old train timetable from 1925 and a violet pastille covered in dust.

She slipped behind the backdrop and made her way back over to Pierre, examining the floor as she walked. She saw nothing but balls of dust and bits of thread.

"I don't suppose you found anything back here?" she asked.

"Just a racing card from Epsom dated from October of last year." He handed it to her and she added it to the stash in her pocket.

"You?"

Imogen told him. "I need to write all this down before I hand over the items to the police."

Pierre lifted one shoulder. "Don't worry. If you let me 'ave a look, I 'ave a bit of a photographic memory."

"Really?" She carefully pulled all the rubbish from her pocket and laid it on her handkerchief in her palms.

He studied the items intensely. "I don't 'ave indefinite recall, but I'll be able to remember them at least until I get 'ome and can write them down."

"How marvelous. That's a talent I would love to have but I fear my memory erodes with each passing year."

Imogen popped the items back into her pocket and headed for the front of the stage where Ophelia and the constable still studied the body.

She caught the end of the constable's sentence. "—until Inspector Southam gets here."

"It's rather untidy up there but I did find some things that may or may not be of interest." She held out the pouch she had made with her handkerchief, and handed over the items she and Pierre had uncovered.

He didn't even look at them, just pushed them into his capacious pocket.

"Can you stay with the body while we wait for the inspector and the doctor? I'd best get a start on interviewing everyone."

As the sisters looked out on the players, almost everyone was sipping hot tea in silence or whimpering. Matilda was in the worst shape, leaning against Patricia and sobbing into a large, man's handkerchief.

"I think I'll use the kitchen as an interview room." Hargrove jumped off the edge of the stage. "Find out who was where when the poor man died."

The constable led a sobbing Matilda to the kitchen, leaving the rest of the cast staring after them in dazed silence.

"What are you thinking?" Imogen asked her sister.

Ophelia sucked in her cheeks. "I think the murderer must not be very bright. They clearly did not think this through."

"I know what you mean." Imogen buried her face in her hands. "It could so easily have been one of the children!"

"Idiot!" Ophelia paced, raking fingers through her hair as she muttered to herself.

Imogen glanced up at her sister. In a very quiet voice, she asked, "Are we in agreement that one of the four leading ladies was the intended target?"

Ophelia pushed up her sleeves, feeling suddenly hot. "I don't think there can be any doubt. That cup contained liquid when it was taken onstage by Alice. And it was the only one. The murderer counted on one of the actresses taking a sip. Then the glass sat in the wings as the promenade scene was carried out. Farmer Jones was just in the wrong place at the wrong time."

Imogen scanned the members of the community theater, searching for any signs of remorse, but every single face showed some degree of shock or fear.

"Kitty is my first guess. She can deny up and down that she was meeting someone in the churchyard at the first practice but I'm no dimwit. I know what I saw. Then I found the recent dog-ends by that tree." Imogen's fingers went to the locket at her neck. "*And* we felt someone watching us as we walked home."

"I think we need to do a deep dive into Miss Fairfax's life." Ophelia bit her lip as she considered.

"But we need to keep an open mind, lovey. It could have been intended for any one of the others, too; Judith, Celina, or Molly. What do we really know about Molly?"

"Indeed." Ophelia crossed her arms. "Could a headmistress with newfangled ideas annoy anyone enough to kill her?"

Imogen ran a worried hand across her brow. "It doesn't seem likely but look how Mildred got her knickers all in a twist about the trousers and self-defense training. Maybe there was someone who felt even more opposed to Judith's new methods."

"True." Ophelia sighed. "The least likely target is Celina, in my opinion."

Imogen wagged a finger. "In all the detective novels it's always the least likely person."

Ophelia frowned. "Need I remind you, this is not a novel."

Though the situation was dire, Imogen felt irritated. "Keep your hair on, lovey!"

"Sorry, ducky." She squeezed Imogen's arm. "This has just really got my goat. What if, as you said, the murderer accidentally killed a child? So reckless. So irresponsible!"

Dr. Pemberton appeared, his brown overcoat wet, the corners of his mouth drawn tight. Huddled groups of costumed performers clutching teacups followed his movements with doleful eyes as he marched straight over to the stage, medical bag in hand.

"Ladies. Why am I not surprised to find you here?" He climbed the steps, setting his bag beside the body. Lifting the sheet he asked, "Who do we have here?"

"It's Farmer Nicholas Jones," said Imogen.

The doctor's face fell. "I just delivered his fourth grandchild last month." He cast a practiced eye over the corpse then began to poke and prod before leaning close to the farmer's face. He lifted one of Nicholas Jones' eyelids, then pressed expert fingers against the neck, examining the pinkish skin.

"Vomitus and almonds," he murmured. "Am I right in guessing that you had already deduced that? Plus, the pink tint to the skin."

"We did," admitted Ophelia. "We think it was administered via a wineglass prop."

"Really? Have you secured the glass for the inspector? What am I saying? Of course you have."

Imogen felt both censured and praised. "You'll be glad to hear we've also kept everyone off the stage and already searched for clues. Pierre Ancien is guarding the area backstage to make sure no one tramples on the scene before the inspector arrives."

"Or comes back to hide the murder weapon," added Ophelia.

"Well, there's no doubt about the time of death since everyone here witnessed the fact. Cyanide works pretty fast, especially on an empty stomach."

Imogen put a finger to her mouth thinking about Farmer Jones' final words before he went onstage. "He may well have skipped dinner to get here as this was our final dress rehearsal and he had been out planting most of the day before coming. That's why he was so thirsty."

"Is cyanide poisoning your official cause of death, doctor?" Ophelia asked, keeping her voice low.

"It is. Jones was a little overweight and didn't get enough sleep, but apart from that, he was in the pink of health. The heavy work of farming kept his muscles strong and his heart in good shape." The doctor raised his head, the skin pulled tight over his jaw. "The thing I can't fathom is why anyone would want to kill him?"

Ophelia shook her head rapidly. "Oh, no, doctor! We believe Farmer Jones was *not* the intended victim. It is our contention that the murderer put the poison in the glass knowing the leading ladies would use them in the dinner scene. Murder is always monstrous, but this takes the biscuit."

He leaned back on his heels. "I see what you mean. *Anyone* could have drunk from that cup. It beggars belief. The killer's thoughtless disregard put everyone in the cast at risk." He looked down at all the people still dressed in their costumes. "Who do you think it was meant to kill?"

Molly had taken off the ridiculous wig and was hugging her boys who both kept their eyes averted from the body on the stage. Kitty and Celina were hunched together in quiet conversation.

"Do you see the lady in the bright pink French gown with those young men? That's Molly Sugden our new confectioner. She has one of the main roles. Then those two ladies over there —" she pointed with her head, "—are also stars of the show. And lastly, our headmistress in the gray dress." Judith was sitting with Alice, her head in her hands. "All those women had a scene at the table immediately prior to the death".

"Well, perhaps we should warn—"

His comments were interrupted by the door crashing against the wall.

Inspector Southam had arrived dressed for the opera.

CHAPTER 10

Curtain Call for Questions

I f the situation had not been so dire, Ophelia would have burst out laughing. The sight of the usually unpretentious inspector crashing into the murder scene in a penguin suit was so completely unexpected. His crisp, white bow tie sat perfectly centered beneath his chin; an opera program still clutched in one hand. Yet somehow, his strikingly elegant attire did not seem entirely out of place among the theatrical costumes surrounding him.

Southam quickly assessed the situation and made for the stage, loosening the snowy white tie.

"You two again? Why can't you just play bridge and drink tea?"

Ophelia smirked. "Where's the fun in that, Inspector?"

Southam turned his attention to the doctor leaning over the dead body.

"Didn't peg you as an opera man," remarked Dr. Pemberton.

The inspector growled. "I'm not! My wife dragged me there. Except for the fact that this poor fellow is dead, I've never been so grateful to be pulled from an event in my life." He pulled out his notebook. Now, what have we here?"

The doctor went through all the facts while the twins looked on.

Southam narrowed his eyes. "And what do you two make of it?"

"Our conclusion is that this death was a mistake and that the killer intended to kill someone else." She explained their reasoning.

Imogen appreciated that the inspector heard them out and did not attempt to interrupt. He had worked with them on several cases now and she believed he had come to respect their opinion.

"And you're sure it's cyanide poisoning?" he asked Pemberton.

"I don't think there's any doubt, but I'll send a sample of his blood to the lab to be tested."

"Right!" He struggled to his feet in black patent dress shoes. "Take me backstage so I can get the lay of the land. Is Constable Hargrove around?"

Imogen gestured in the direction of the kitchen. "He's taking witness statements in the kitchen, Inspector."

"When he comes out, kindly let him know I'm here."

Imogen took the inspector into the wings, while Ophelia stayed with the doctor.

"We asked Mr. Ancien, there, to secure the back of the stage in case the murderer returned." She waved at Pierre and the inspector nodded in his direction. "And I gave some items of interest I found to the constable for safekeeping."

Giving her the side eye, the inspector chewed the inside of his mouth. "Where were you standing when the chap keeled over?"

"I'm in charge of wardrobe as well as being the prop manager. My other job was prompter. So, I stood right here to be able to be in all those places." She took him to where she was standing. "Pierre was working the lights just there." She pointed to the panel next to the curtain.

"And where was the wineglass?"

"The pirates' chorus had just run the table offstage and placed it here." She leaned on the table. "The glasses were still on top. They were all supposed to be empty for rehearsal but one of them was full and spilled on Mrs. Puddingfield's dress. We thought nothing of it at the time."

He touched the remaining glasses with the end of his pencil. "I assume you gave the glass with the poison to Hargrove?"

"I did. As soon as we realized the cause of death, we removed that wineglass from the set. There are children around and we didn't want another accident."

He moved to where Imogen was standing. "The table was placed just like this?"

"Yes. We've not moved it."

"And there were four glasses for the four actresses?"

"Correct."

He wrote something in his book. "Where was Farmer Jones?"

"He was a bit late to practice. He had to go on for a scene as soon as he got here, then he disappeared again. He hurried up those stairs and into the wings just next to me for his big scene with the solo." She pointed to the stairs at the back of the stage.

"Why was he late?"

"It's sowing season. He wanted to get all the planting done before the weather changed. I could tell he was harried because his cheeks were flushed, and his brow was damp. When he caught sight of the water in the glass, he swigged the lot then ran on for his bit. Within seconds, he gurgled and gasped, clutching his throat, then sank to the floor twitching in a most alarming fashion. Matilda thought he was fooling around at first."

Southam leaned against the table. "Who else was on this side?"

Imogen listed off the people. "But the pertinent fact is that the table and glasses came on from the *other* side. The ladies' chorus carried the props on stage. The men's chorus carried them off."

He squinted. "So, who was on the other side?"

Imogen closed her eyes and thought back. "Prudence Cresswell, the vicar's wife, she's the prop manager and prompter on that side. The ladies' chorus consisted of Mildred Chumbley, Alice Puddingfield, Patricia Snodgrass and Sally Pratt. Ed Sugden was also on that side in case any of the scenery needed fixing." She tapped her lips. "The four leading ladies were Celina

Sutherland, Judith Rutherford, Molly Sugden and Kitty Fairfax. The last two have recently moved to the village."

Southam checked his notes. "Where was your sister?"

"She was at the piano down there. And Matilda Butterworth is the director, so she was down on the floor too."

"Were the props here long before the practice started?"

"Not really. They were brought from various places right before the start of rehearsal and gathered on each side."

Southam went quiet for a while. "So, are you saying that only those taking part in the production could have put the poison in the glass."

Imogen felt a jolt. "I suppose I am." She had a thought. "The caretaker was here at the beginning too, but he left right after we started the rehearsal."

"Well, that narrows it down nicely." He put the pencil in his breast pocket. "If you don't mind, I'm going to have a poke about."

"Of course." She gestured to Pierre and they both descended from the small stage.

The doctor had covered the body again while they waited for more police officers to arrive.

"Does Southam agree with our deduction?" Ophelia asked as Pierre slipped his arm through hers.

"He's being a bit tightlipped, but he did say that since the prop glasses arrived right before the start of the rehearsal and no one else came in, the murderer must have been someone in the room."

Ophelia's bottom lip shrugged. "He's right. And that always makes me feel jittery. Someone in here is a murderer." She clamped Pierre's arm in hers. "Is the inspector going to share the bad news with the leading ladies?"

"He didn't tell me. But he'll have to at some point. I'm just worried it might lead to more hysteria if he tells them now."

Matilda, looking worse for wear, stumbled out of the kitchen. Ophelia pushed Pierre in her direction. He helped her onto a chair while Ophelia got her another cup of tea.

"He wants Kitty next," Matilda managed to croak.

"I'll let her know."

Ophelia approached the two friends and was shocked to find Kitty trembling, the black mascara halfway down her cheeks. Her wild hair had broken free of its chains. Gone was the beautiful transformation they had all witnessed an hour ago.

"The constable would like to see you for questioning, Kitty."

The girl's reaction was startling – not just nervous, she was terrified. Her hands flew to her throat still clutching the blotchy handkerchief. "Why me? Why now?"

"No particular reason," Ophelia said carefully, watching as Kitty's fingers twisted the cloth. "He's working his way through everyone."

"But there are so many others," Kitty whispered, her eyes darting to the kitchen door. "Surely someone else could go first?" A rabbit in a trap came to mind.

"But he asked for you. I wouldn't read too much into it."

Kitty stared at Celina. "Can't you come with me?"

"Uh—" Celina shifted uncomfortably in her chair.

"I'm afraid that's not how it works," intervened Ophelia. "But Constable Hargrove is a very nice man. He won't bite."

Kitty rose unsteadily, seeming more like a child than a grown woman.

Ophelia took her seat. "She seems to have taken this hard."

"It's not every day you watch a man die right in front of you," observed Celina.

"True." Ophelia looked around the hall at all the subdued people. "What do you know about Kitty?"

Celina tutted. "Not you as well?"

"What do you mean?"

"All the locals have been eyeing her because she's a recent arrival." The librarian huffed with irritation.

Ophelia lifted up both palms. "I can assure you that's not what I meant."

"No." Celina exhaled. "Sorry. I'm a bit shaken myself."

Ophelia put a hand on her shoulder. "It would be more strange if you weren't, ducky."

"It's no excuse for snapping at you like that. I'm sorry." Celina crossed her legs and arms. "I know Kitty's from a large family near Birmingham and I know she was the first in her family to get an education."

That much Ophelia already knew. "I don't suppose she had a young man or anything since she moved all the way down here."

Celina caught Ophelia's eye. "Why do I get the feeling you already know that she did?"

Ophelia struggled to hold back a smile. "She might have told me about a certain young fellow who broke it off after she finished college. Thought she was too good for him with all her learning. I was wondering if you knew any more about him?"

Celina sniffed. "I know he didn't end up marrying that girl he was carrying on with."

"I wonder why?" mused Ophelia.

"There was some kind of scandal, but Kitty wouldn't tell me what." She wiped under her eye and smudged mascara across her cheek.

With Celina's attention captured, Ophelia seized the chance to ask some questions relating to the case. "Did you notice anything unusual before rehearsal began?"

"Are you kidding? There was hardly room for all of us in our big dresses, what with the props and scenery and everything. We were like sardines in a tin."

Ophelia had to concede that would have been the case on both sides. It was a big production on a small stage. But this also meant that anyone could have slipped the poison into a glass without being noticed.

"I didn't say anything to Kitty," began Celina, "but I couldn't help noticing you, Imogen and the doctor talking. I could tell by your faces that the farmer's death wasn't natural. I just keep wondering who would want to kill poor Nicholas Jones. That man wouldn't hurt a fly. He even dressed up as Father Christmas last year, for the children at the library."

Ophelia chose not to use this opening to share their current theory on the murder. Instead, she agreed with Celina. "It does look that way, I'm afraid. I'm sure the police will tell us more in time." She stood. "I'd best check on everyone else."

As Ophelia moved over to the corner that held Judith and Alice, the headmistress's head snapped up with expectation. "Do you know anything, Miss Harrington?"

"Not much more than you, I'm sure."

Judith's head shook. "Please be honest with me. Alice and I have been talking. She's told me about all the crimes you've solved since moving here and I've been watching your sister and the inspector. The way they've been searching the stage …" She wiped her nose. "It's like you don't think he died of a heart attack or something."

Ophelia still hesitated.

"I think we have a right to know," added Alice. "We were witnesses, after all."

Ophelia shrugged. "There is some concern of causing a panic."

"If I promise to remain calm, and not tell anyone else, will you be honest with me?" asked the headmistress.

Ophelia weighed the options. Judith had been perceptive enough to notice the beginnings of an investigation just like Celina. But Ophelia sensed her intelligence had taken the headmistress even further. "I will need your word."

Judith and Alice put their hands over their hearts.

"Nicholas Jones was poisoned," she said softly.

The two women's eyes flared with disbelief.

"I was still hoping it was a heart attack—the way he clutched his chest," gasped Alice.

Ophelia glanced around the room to ensure that no one else was listening. "I'm afraid not. There are other indicators of poisoning."

Judith shrank into her chair. "It was bad enough that someone died in front of me but knowing he was murdered is so much worse."

"The doctor and the inspector both agree on the cause of death."

Judith's face crumpled. "Is this village cursed?"

"It does seem that way," said Alice patting Judith's back.

"And Alice, the police will need your dress for testing." The baker glanced down at the gown that had now dried but showed slight stains.

"The poison was in the water?"

"Yep."

"But—"

"Do you have other clothes?" Ophelia cut Alice off before she could draw another conclusion and scare the poor headmistress out of her mind.

"Uh, yes. Shall I change now?"

"That might be a good idea."

Alice stood and walked a few steps keeping her eyes on Ophelia's before finally turning to go to the ladies' toilet.

"I saw a lot of horrible things when I was a nurse in the war, but this? The idea that one of our friends poisoned another. It's terrifying." Judith seemed to be having trouble holding onto her emotions.

"I completely agree."

Ophelia studied the rest of the actors again. Reggie was drumming his fingers frantically against his striped pirate trousers, the rhythm matching the ticking of the hall clock. His usual sunny disposition had evaporated completely. In the corner, Des attempted to maintain his composure as he continued to comfort Matilda.

"His time was just up, that's all. Could have been any of us older ones ..." But Des's words rang hollow in the tense atmosphere.

Young Tommy kept tugging at his collar as if it were choking him, while Collin rocked in his chair. Patricia's fingers mechanically smoothed non-existent wrinkles from her skirt. Everyone was on pins and needles.

"Stop right there!" Southam's command cracked through the air like a whip. The inspector moved with surprising agility for a middle-aged man in evening dress, crossing the space in three long strides.

Imogen's head jerked around to see Mildred, frozen, holding a brown bottle that shook in her hand like a confession. Behind her, the bathroom door swung slowly shut, creaking as it did so into the sudden silence that had fallen over the hall.

"Don't move!" Southam reiterated, pulling a handkerchief from his breast pocket. "And for heaven's sake, don't drop it!"

CHAPTER 11

Midnight Musings

T he inspector reached for the brown bottle wearing gloves. "Where did you find this?"

"I had just finished using the lavatory when I noticed my earring had come loose. I tried to tighten it, but it dropped into the bin," responded Mildred. "I reached down and my hands hit this. I thought it might be important."

"I would advise you to wash your hands again, Miss Chumbley."

Mildred hesitated.

"Now, Miss Chumbley."

She pivoted and returned to the ladies' room.

Ophelia approached the inspector who showed her the plain bottle.

"Too bad it doesn't bear a poison label, but I'll send it for testing. If this *is* the cyanide bottle, we're lucky we didn't have multiple deaths tonight."

By the time the police had taken away the body and interviewed everyone, it was after midnight. Alice had discreetly removed her costume, placed the dress in a bag and slipped it to Ophelia. She handed the poisoned gown to the inspector.

"No need to clean up yet," Southam told Matilda. "I'll have my men go over everything with a fine-tooth comb."

Matilda, who was still traumatized, merely nodded and let Des lead her home.

Pierre accompanied the twins to Badger's Hollow. The walk home took on an eerie quality as the moonlight caught the ripples on the pond's surface where a frosty March breeze stirred the water. Even the usually welcoming crescent of cottages seemed ominous in the shadowy night, their windows mostly dark except for the odd gleam of lamplight.

When the three of them reached the curve in the lane where Badger's Hollow lay, Imogen paused, looking back across the green toward the village hall. Police lanterns glimmered, bobbing in the darkness like cinders from a fire.

The events of the evening had transformed their familiar little village into something dubious, something less certain. Every rustle in the reeds around the pond, every creak of a gate along the way home seemed to whisper that another tragedy had occurred.

"Would you like to come in for a hot drink?" Ophelia asked Pierre while Tiger lost his mind on the other side of the door.

"I'm all done up," he said, the lines on his face more pronounced this evening.

This earned a small grin from the twins. "It's, 'done in', not 'done up'," said Ophelia. He responded by touching the tip of her nose, tipping his hat and marching down the garden path. They waited before letting the dog out to do his business. He had been on his own for much longer than usual. Imogen fumbled twice with the door key before managing to unlock it, her usually steady hands betraying her weariness.

Tiger bolted past them then reappeared, his tail wagging with fury and his head burrowing into Imogen's legs.

"Come in, boy."

They made their way straight to the kitchen's cozy comfort with its perpetually ticking clock above the Aga, copper pots above the table and stack of well-worn teacups on their hooks. The protection and security the space offered tonight was especially welcome.

While Imogen measured Horlicks into the mugs – the blue ones their mother had always insisted made hot drinks taste better – Ophelia sat heavily in her customary chair, absently rubbing the knot that had formed in her neck from hours of tension. The simple task of untying her shoes seemed monumental.

Imogen filled the dog's water bowl, fed him a treat and put the milk on the stove to boil before slumping into another chair at the battered kitchen table.

"Well, that didn't go quite as expected," said Imogen with a lop-sided smile.

"That might be the understatement of the year." She leaned back to stretch her arms. "I don't envy Inspector Southam having to tell Mrs. Jones why her husband didn't come home."

"I imagine that's the worst part of their job," agreed Imogen.

"You don't have any ideas who did it, do you?" Though Ophelia had more skills in the actual investigative process, Imogen was the one who experienced bursts of insight that finally solved their cases.

Imogen spread her hands on the time-worn table. "I'm at a loss. I've gone over and over everything in my head a dozen times, but I didn't see anyone acting suspiciously." She pulled her fingers into fists. "But the thing that's really bothering me is that someone expected a death tonight, just not the one that happened. They're going to try again."

Ophelia's face stretched into an expression of bewilderment. "It must have been an incredible shock when they watched Farmer Jones go down instead of one of the ladies."

Imogen huffed. "*That* might be the understatement of the year."

"The problem was that everyone appeared horrified. Witnessing death will do that to a person."

"Even so, Kitty's reaction did seem extreme to me," Imogen

murmured, rubbing her hands together in the chilly kitchen. "Even for someone experiencing their first violent death."

"She's been on edge ever since the incident with the dark stranger, if you ask me," Ophelia pointed out. "She was quite a different person before he came along. We should ask Celina if she's noticed a change in her." Ophelia sat up straighter. "She denied it completely, didn't she? The meeting with the dark figure, I mean. But why lie? Unless ..." Her voice trailed off as she considered the implications.

Imogen brushed some crumbs from the table. "We know almost nothing about Kitty's life in Birmingham. Just that she grew up there in a large family and had that broken engagement."

"Which ended badly enough for her to move clear across the country." Ophelia reached for a pencil and paper.

Imogen snapped her fingers. "I've just had a thought. Remember how good she is at accents. She may not even be *from* Birmingham!"

Ophelia pursed her lips as she considered Imogen's comment. "That would be easy enough to check. We can ask Patricia if she gets mail from there."

Imogen went to check on the milk. Seeing it bubbling at the edges, she poured the hot liquid into the mugs.

"Did you tell anyone we suspect the wrong person died?" She began to stir each cup and went to add a teaspoon of sugar to both, nearly missing the second mug entirely. A small cascade of sugar crystals scattered across the worn wooden counter. She put her lack of precision down to the lateness of the hour and the weight of the day's events.

"When did we last eat?" Ophelia wondered aloud, though making toast seemed an insurmountable task. She settled for nudging the biscuit tin closer to her sister, but neither of them made any effort to open it.

"I wasn't going to tell anyone anything before they'd been questioned by the police in case it muddied the water, but Judith is no fool and realized that the presence of the inspector meant it wasn't just a heart attack. Then when I asked Alice to give her dress to the police, she put two and two together, but I shut her down pretty quickly and she got the message."

"I bet she's telling Archie all about it now."

Imogen handed a mug to Ophelia then took her seat across the table, hands wrapped around her own cup, soaking in the lovely warmth and considering the biscuit tin.

"Let's review the leading ladies as potential victims," suggested Ophelia, taking a sip. "The only long-term resident of the village is Celina. Though she was the secret love-interest of the verger, before he died, she was also the niece of a murderer. Could she have been the target of someone who was affected by her aunt's crimes?"

Imogen put down her mug and tickled Tiger behind the ears. "Most of the people involved in that investigation are dead or live in Wiltshire. We would certainly have noticed a complete stranger, even in all that chaos."

"True. And I hardly think anyone would go to the lengths of poisoning someone over library fines."

Imogen was too tired to laugh, though she did find her sister's comment funny.

"Judith. She's earned her stripes by wrangling the school into order. Augusta Trumble was organized but she was a disciple of the old ways. That said, I just don't see anyone getting so upset with new methods that they would poison the headmistress."

"Much more likely to storm the governor's meeting and demand her removal," said Imogen with a lazy chuckle.

"Or, if they were particularly incensed, accost her at the school."

"Everyone I've talked to, except Mildred, showers her with praise. Even the students in the reception class are reading, I've been told."

The dog struggled to his furry feet on the flagstone floor and helped himself to a great deal of water which sloshed over the sides of his bowl as his tongue worked overtime, creating puddles that spread across the ancient stones.

Ophelia continued. "Then there's the real newcomers; Molly and Kitty. As you pointed out, what do we really know about them? Only what they have told us." She played with the fringe of a place mat that was centered on the table under a vase of dried flowers.

"I read a book a couple of months ago where one of the characters arrived in a new town and completely re-invented themselves," murmured Imogen. "How do we know they haven't done the same thing?"

Ophelia thumped the table causing Tiger to lift his head with interest. "We don't. They could tell us anything about their past and we would believe it. We may have to make a trip to Manchester and Birmingham."

Imogen frowned. "It will be horribly cold and wet at this time of year."

"True. Let's start closer to home. Kitty is a teacher at Willowbrook school. We can try to talk with the other teachers or villagers, without being obvious, of course."

"I see a lot of tea in our future." Imogen had given up trying to sit properly, sprawling sideways in her chair, head propped awkwardly on her hand. A loose strand of hair had escaped her usually neat bun, but she seemed beyond noticing or caring.

"Not necessarily. We could catch them in all sorts of places like the baker's or butcher's. We can engage them in conversation and see if what she told *us* is the same as what she told *them*."

"That might work." Imogen could feel her lids dropping and was losing the will to fight them.

"Lastly, Molly. It's a long way from Manchester. Why move so far from friends and family?"

"Why, indeed?" slurred Imogen as she lost the battle with fatigue.

"Perhaps it was trouble with family, or a scandal?" Imogen's eyes were closed. "But you're exhausted. Go on up to bed. I'm going to sit and think for a while."

"Alright, if you insist. Tiger will appreciate the company." As Imogen drained her mug, she thought of something else. "I overheard David Sugden telling Reggie he missed his old cricket club. Said the matches there were more 'exciting' – whatever that means. Which makes me wonder even more why they moved away at all." She pushed down on the tabletop to winch herself to standing, then stumbled out of the kitchen like a sleepwalker, and up the stairs. A *thump* indicated she had fallen into bed without washing her face.

"What do *you* think?" Ophelia asked the dog, who tipped his head and perked his ears, thick tail whumping the floor. "I think we should start with the outsiders. And that's just to discover who was supposed to die tonight." She shivered. "But without knowing that, I fear we will fail to find the murderer."

She ran through the names of all the people present at the rehearsal, shaking her head that any of them could murder another in cold blood. In a flash, she remembered that Pierre had committed all the potential clues Imogen had found on the stage and in the wings, to memory and scribbled them down for her before they left for home. She shuffled down the hall to find the paper in her coat pocket.

The dog welcomed her back to the kitchen as if she had been gone for three months. It took some time to calm him and lead him back to his place near the stove. She poured a dash of milk into his food bowl.

Sitting at the table she ran an eye over the list.

The items that most caught her interest were the cigarette stub, the fragment of a telegram, the pawn ticket, the matchbook from Parkford, the train timetable, and the racing card. Each item could be innocent stage detritus, of course, or they could be breadcrumbs leading to their killer.

She tapped the paper with her finger. Hadn't Imogen said the stranger with Kitty had left a pile of cigarette ends by an oak tree? If memory served, Imogen had pocketed one. The cigarette stub found on stage might connect Kitty's mysterious visitor to the crime. "I wonder if any of the cast members smoke? It might be worth checking," she mused.

In the morning, she would ask Imogen about it. Perhaps they

could compare the brands of the dog end found on the stage and the one she had brought home. She sighed. The fact was that lots of people smoked these days, even women. It might be a dead end.

Moving on, she considered the words Pierre had seen on the fragment of telegram. There was no year, but the date was early February and the few tantalizing words were, 'expect me no—'. The words nagged at her. It could be 'noon'? Or perhaps 'not'? Or 'no later than', as well as a hundred other possibilities. And who was expecting whom?

The train timetable was old but did the times really change from year to year? She could ask the inspector if the paper showed *where* the timetable was purchased.

Pierre had written that the racing card was from Doncaster, November of 1928. Just a few months ago. She thought Doncaster was in the Midlands. She would need to check.

The pawn ticket, though trampled and dirty, seemed the most promising lead. It was from Parkford and was recent. She and Imogen had trolled the pawn shops in the county seat of Parkford in their second case. She pulled up a vivid image of the Dickensian owner of *Humble Henry's Hock* and smiled to herself. Looked like they would be paying Henry another visit.

And while they were in Parkford, they could visit *The Lion Hotel*. It was a mid-range establishment, not too expensive but with a good reputation for quality. Many commercial salesmen used it. They should make that one of their first ports of call to check out the hotel's current match books.

As the clock struck two, Tiger's pig-like snore reminded her of the late hour.

Time for bed.

CHAPTER 12

Letters and Lies

After Ophelia had discussed her thoughts from the night before with Imogen over breakfast, her sister retrieved the cigarette end she had found by the tree. "We can take this to Constable Hargrove for comparison with the one I found on the stage."

The possibility of this connection to Kitty helped them decide to postpone their trip to Parkford in favor of a shopping trip to Willowbrook to learn more about Kitty's past.

Though rain pounded their windows, they remained undeterred. Donning rubber boots, macintoshes and umbrellas they plodded their way through the puddles to the bus stop for the half-past nine bus to the neighboring village of Willowbrook.

Ophelia settled onto the bench seat of the bus, holding the dripping umbrella away from her stockinged legs. "Here's the plan. It might be difficult to intercept the teachers during the day and we can't exactly go marching into the school, so I thought we could visit the different shop owners, act naturally and simply pass the time of day. I'm sure the gossip mill is as active here as in Saffron Weald. If that fails, we can try another strategy."

Imogen shook her umbrella and the raindrops slid to the ground, forming a pool of water by her feet. "What's our ruse? It's going to look rather odd showing up to shop in a different village."

"I gave a lot of thought to this while I was getting ready for bed last night. Willowbrook has a haberdasher, and we don't. We can say we came to get notions for our costumes."

"Oh, that's good. But what if they've already heard about the murder and are shocked we're still going to perform the play?"

"First of all, since the murder only happened last night, I doubt that news of it will have spread yet. Plus, since Farmer Jones was killed accidentally, the police have probably not reported it to the media. And why shouldn't we perform the play after a decent period of mourning? Life must go on."

Imogen gazed out the window. "If you say so."

The bus dropped them at the top of the high street. Willowbrook only dated back two hundred years, and the architecture was less uniform than in Saffron Weald. Instead of thatch, the roofs were made of gray slate, the buildings a patchwork of different designs.

As they walked, large drops pelted the pavement, and finding their way to the haberdasher they hurried in out of the storm.

A thin man with a pot belly dropped the spool of thread he was holding as they approached. "H-how do you do?" His pencil thin mustache wiggled as his eyes snapped between the identical women before him. "And how may I help you?"

"We're on the hunt for ribbon for several costumes."

"Am I in the presence of thespians?" His lips bunched tight like a vole.

"Dear me, no!" laughed Imogen. "My sister here plays the piano for our current production, and I manage the backstage stuff which includes the costumes."

"Ah. I understand. Let me show you our ribbon rack." Clasping his hands in front of his chest, he came around the counter. "Here we are. Every color of the rainbow. What is the production, if I may ask?"

"*The Pirate's Fiancée*," Imogen responded.

"Oh! If I'm not mistaken, our little Miss Fairfax is in that production. You must be from Saffron Weald."

This was easier than Ophelia had even hoped. "As a matter of fact, we are. Miss Fairfax has such a lovely voice. We couldn't help but put her in the lead role. Plus, she said she'd been in several school productions back in Birmingham."

The haberdasher stiffened. "I believe you misspoke, madam. Miss Fairfax is from Liverpool."

Ophelia flared her eyes at Imogen before saying, "Oh, yes. Silly me. It's all 'up north' to me."

"It's a common mistake," he agreed while pulling on several rolls of ribbon.

"She's superb in the role though. I hope you'll come and watch. She becomes quite a different person on stage." *And apparently in her real life.*

"My wife is fond of the theater. Perhaps we will. When will it be playing?"

Imogen began picking up some loose buttons. "The date hasn't been quite fixed yet. We're still in rehearsal." She raised her gaze to his, holding several buttons in her hand. "I wonder if any of her family will come down to watch?"

Fiddling with a length of ribbon, his face creased into a frown. "Family? But don't you know? She has none. They were all killed in a fire while she was away at teacher training college. So tragic."

The information the haberdasher relayed was astonishing. "Oh, dear. You'll have to excuse us. She's only been a resident of our village for a month or two. We're still getting to know her."

His eyelids fluttered. "Lovely girl, though. The children at the school adore her."

The twins chose two types of ribbon, asking for three yards of each as they digested the staggering information. While the haberdasher laid the ribbon against the yard stick built into the counter, he chattered on in his clipped voice about the weather and how he was looking forward to spring.

Ophelia counted out the coins from her purse and shot one last arrow. "Did we hear correctly that Miss Fairfax had been engaged?"

His mustache stilled. "Now, in that you are correct. I understand he was a bit of a rough fellow, and after college, Miss Fairfax had become more refined. They were no longer suited, and she broke it off. That's why she took a job so far away. Put some distance between them." He rolled up the ribbon and slipped it into a white paper bag. Taking the coins from Ophelia, he slid them into the cash register.

He pulled down on the waistcoat that tried to cover his protruding belly. "Come back any time. Our prices are much better than the places in Parkford.

The sisters smiled and almost ran out of the store.

"Well, your theory about reinventing herself was spot on, ducky. Nothing of what she told us is true. Nothing."

Arriving back in Saffron Weald, they spent lunchtime describing their visit to Pierre.

"That does make 'er the most likely to 'ave a past that may 'ave followed 'er 'ere."

"We're on the same wavelength," said Ophelia. "But now we have to figure out a way to confront Kitty about her lies. She was pretty fragile yesterday."

"May I suggest you leave that to the police?"

"You are at liberty to suggest it, Mr. Ancien, but we are free to dismiss your proposal."

He winked. "I should have known."

"However, I do think we should give Kitty a little time to recover from last night's ordeal, which is why I suggest we all go to Parkford this afternoon to follow up on that pawnshop ticket."

"Pierre, you wrote down some information from the torn stub," began Imogen. "But we were wondering if you can recall anything about the shop name. I vaguely remember a blue 'a' and 'r' but I'm not absolutely sure."

Pierre pondered. "It *was* blue print, but I believe it was a 'c' and a 'k'.

Ophelia jumped out of her seat. "Hock!" she squealed. "*Humble Henry's Hock.*"

Imogen shrank as the image of horrible Henry, as she called him, swam before her eyes. "Not *him.*"

"I'll come with you," declared Pierre, and Imogen immediately felt better about a visit to the seedy shop and its greasy owner.

The sizable market town of Parkford, county seat of Meadowshire, was quite old. It had started life as a watering hole for coach drivers and expanded over the centuries with no master plan in mind.

The pawn shop was in a dark side alley where undesirables loitered in doorways. As Pierre parked his car, he let out a bark of laughter.

"No wonder Imogen was scared. This place is the very definition of squalid. Should I be worried about my car?"

Ophelia swatted his arm. "Don't be silly. We'll only be here a minute and then we're off to *The Lion.*"

The three of them entered the dingy, smelly store where the hulking figure of the grubby broker emerged out of the gloom.

Imogen's nose wrinkled. They had been here twice before, once to pawn something in order to question the proprietor, and the second time, to retrieve her beloved gray pearl once the case had been solved. She had hated each visit with a passion and would never forget the pungent aroma of death mixed with tobacco and dirt.

Ophelia took great delight in watching Pierre's expression of unbelief as the Fagin-like broker turned weepy eyes on the trio.

"Ah," he began in that wheezy, scratchy voice. "'Ow could I forget the gray pearl ladies?"

Clearly, he remembered what customers brokered, rather than their names. "I see you brought a friend." His lips pulled back like a dog baring its teeth but Ophelia realized it was actually a smile revealing filthy, broken teeth.

Imogen took an involuntary step back.

"This is our friend Marcel," lied Ophelia as Pierre seemed oddly tongue-tied. "He has an interest in antiques."

Henry opened his fingers in a chef's kiss and squinted. "Oh, yeah? Plenty o' those in 'ere, mate."

Pierre failed to cover up a snort of derision but pretended to cough.

One weepy eye closed, while the other examined Pierre closely. Pierre straightened his hat and stared at his shoes.

Henry's gaze idled over to Ophelia and he rubbed dirty hands together in the fingerless gloves she remembered so well. "What can I do for you today, then?"

"Actually, we're interested in an item that may have been pawned quite recently."

The rheumy eyes narrowed. "Need a ticket."

"I'm afraid we don't have that but we do have the last three digits of the stub; 754."

Pulling a battered ledger toward him with soiled fingers, he flicked the pages with broken nails and ran them down a page. "754?"

"That's right."

Flicking the long, lanky hair out of his face, he rubbed his bulbous nose as his eyebrows danced. "Wot's it worth to ya?"

Did this mean he had the item and knew who had pawned it? Ophelia's heart raced.

"I might be interested in purchasing the item."

Henry's bottom lip came up to cover his broken teeth and his nose dipped down to greet it. "Oh, yeah?" He cackled like a witch. "'Old on a mo."

Henry shuffled into the back room, his wheezing laugh echoing off the grimy walls. After a few moments, a strange sound emanated from the depths of the store, like someone dragging a dead body along the ground. The three stared at each other with puzzled expressions. What could it be?

Henry emerged from the back room dragging a severely

battered, gentleman's travel trunk.

"'Ere you are, then." Henry was clearly having fun at their expense.

"Uh—how much do you want for it?" Ophelia tried to sound as though it was exactly what she had expected.

"The bloke wot dropped it off 'as twenty more days to claim it." Henry thumbed his nose waiting for her reaction.

"Oh."

Pierre came to the rescue. "'Ow much would it cost to just take a quick peek inside. I'm sure we can come to an agreement of some kind."

"An agreement of some kind ..." Henry mimicked Pierre's accent then his face underwent a startling transformation, the mocking grin collapsed into cold calculation as swiftly as a door slamming shut. "Now that's a different matter entirely, ain't it, guv?"

"Would £5 do the trick?" Pierre was already pulling out his wallet.

Ophelia noticed the slightest flaring of the odious nostrils.

"Ten."

Her hackles rose. "Now you're just being greedy, Henry." She spun to face Imogen and slipped her arm through Pierre's as if to leave, but it was all part of the game, a game she had learned well in Morocco.

"Seven." His tone showed he had no intention of losing such a high sum without having to sell anything.

"£6, two and six. Final offer." Ophelia's tone was rigid.

"Done!" He fished in his saggy jacket pocket for the key and handed it over while Pierre gave him the agreed upon amount.

Ophelia briefly examined the key. It was not unlike the one they had found in the clock but this one was larger and plain.

Henry leaned against the wall, legs and arms crossed, watching them. "Ain't much in it."

So, he had not been above snooping himself.

The trunk looked as though it had been hauled out of a rubbish tip. A monogram of F and R in beautiful, intertwined rolling script was almost illegible. She turned the key in the lock, glancing at her sister as she did so.

Henry was right, there wasn't much in it. On the top lay a scruffy, folded jacket that she held up for Pierre to take. Underneath the jacket sat a stack of letters tied with a stained ribbon. The envelopes were addressed to a village in Liverpool. She gave those to Imogen. Next was a dog-eared photograph of some children. Several of the faces had been scratched out with something sharp.

Digging further, her fingers touched a ring box. Her expectations soared but on opening the box, her hopes were dashed as the box proved to be empty. Right at the bottom she found a slip of paper formally sacking someone from a Liverpool shipping company. The name of the man was Jack Scroggins. Lastly, at the very bottom were some old train timetables from Liverpool to various places in England.

"These letters are from Kitty," said Imogen, thumbing through the pages. "The juvenile handwriting appears rather old as the ink has faded, but they aren't dated."

Ophelia leaned back on her haunches. "Well, that's something. It shows a connection between Kitty and this Jack fellow, and means this trunk likely belongs to the stranger you saw her with. And now we know his name." She waved the job termination letter. "This is evidence he lost his job on the docks. He could be desperate and has come to Kitty for money."

"I'm even more eager to have a sit down with our Miss Fairfax. She's lied to all of us, and I want to know why," declared Imogen, ire rising in her chest.

"What does she say in the letters?" asked Pierre.

"It's all lovey-dovey stuff that young people say to each other. As far as I can see, there's nothing of substance here, certainly nothing referring to the broken engagement. I think the letters pre-date that event."

"Per'aps she still 'as the ring and 'e 'as come to recover it to fund 'is living expenses. That would explain the empty ring box."

"True," agreed Ophelia.

She examined the photographs. "Henry, can I borrow your eye glass?"

He narrowed his eyes. "Who are you people really? You're not just nosy neighbors. Come on, out with it!"

Imogen said the first thing that came to mind. "We're private detectives. Our client is searching for a missing person and a ticket stub from your establishment brought us here."

Despite his best efforts to disguise it, Henry was impressed, evidenced by the elevation of his sagging brow. "You think the bloke wot brought it here is the missing fella?"

"It's certainly possible." Ophelia pushed on the chest to stand up.

Henry offered her the grubby magnifier which she cleaned with her handkerchief before putting it to her own eye.

The photograph was of a group of children dressed for school. She peered closer and her brain fired with recognition. "I think this is a young Kitty." She passed the picture to Imogen.

"Although the print is small and a bit blurry, I can see evidence of her frizzy hair. What do *you* think?" Imogen delivered both items to Pierre.

"Possibly." He passed the photograph back to Ophelia who studied the children whose faces had been obliterated. It was a boy and a girl. The picture had to be over eight years old, going by the outdated fashion of the clothing. The boys would have changed beyond recognition.

She returned all the items to the box and locked it. "Can you tell us the name of the person who brought this to you?" Hopefully it was Jack Scroggins, but she did not want to make unsubstantiated assumptions.

"'E just wrote 'is initials. Some people likes their privacy."

"And what were those?" Ophelia was losing her patience.

"It weren't the same as on that trunk, I can tell you that. Let me see." He referred to the ledger. "'J', 'S' is wot 'e wrote in me book." He clasped his hands on the smudged counter.

Ophelia's pulse gave a little jump.

Hello, Jack Scroggins.

CHAPTER 13

The Lion Hotel

T he Lion Hotel, built as a private residence for the mayor of Parkford in the early eighteenth century, sat just off the main square of the town. It was an impressive square structure formed from white limestone that had weathered to a soft honey color over the centuries. A brass lion's head door knocker held pride of place on the heavy oak front door, worn to a dull sheen by generations of visitors' hands.

The mayor's death had cost his heirs dearly in taxes, necessitating that the family sell the house. After passing from pillar to post until the late 1800s, the grand house was finally purchased by a business-minded hotelier. He renovated from top to bottom, dividing each room into two smaller rooms, thus doubling the occupancy capacity. In line with more modern thinking, he also provided a restaurant rather than a kitchen and set his cap at gentleman farmers. Now, in 1929, it catered to traveling salesmen.

Inside, the hotel lobby – the former grand entryway of the mayor's residence – retained echoes of its former splendor. The new owners had kept the original flagstone floors, now softened by scattered Persian rugs in rich jewel tones. A mahogany reception desk, dark with age and polish, dominated one wall, while brass sconces cast a warm glow over wood-paneled walls. The air held hints of delicious cooking aromas from the restaurant beyond.

Pierre approached the desk where a young woman sat beneath an ornate gilt-framed mirror that reflected the afternoon light, the twins standing a little behind him as if they were not together. Ophelia whispered to Pierre that he could have the stage.

"Bonjour!" He flashed the young receptionist his most disarming smile.

She buckled, batting her eyelashes before becoming distracted by the sight of identical twins. "How can I help you, sir?"

Pierre removed the matchbook from his pocket, holding it out for her to see. "I found these at my cousin's apartment and thought that if 'e liked this 'otel so much, I might give it a try since I 'appen to be in the area."

The young woman glanced at the matches. "Oh, yes. We changed to that matchbook design at the beginning of the year, sir."

"I was 'oping you could show me a room before I make a final decision."

She offered him a winsome smile. "Let me ring for someone."

This was *not* the result the twins were hoping for. They needed the receptionist to leave the desk so they could take a peek in the register.

Pierre tried another tack. "Per'aps, before I look at the accommodations, you could show me the restaurant. I often judge an establishment by the food."

The petite, blonde girl hesitated. Pierre turned on the charm again and she capitulated.

She looked past his shoulder to the twins. "Do you mind waiting while I show this gentleman to the restaurant? I won't be long."

"Not at all," replied Imogen. "You do what you need to do. We're in no hurry."

"If anyone comes in while I'm gone, can you tell them I'll be back in a tick—" the receptionist remembered her manners, "—moment."

"Of course." Imogen arranged her features into a grandmotherly smile.

As soon as the receptionist left, Imogen stood in front of the desk, blocking it from view, while Ophelia ran behind, grabbing the register and dropping to the floor. Imogen kept her eyes peeled for any staff.

Running her fingers down the pages, Ophelia made it three pages back when she made a significant discovery and let out an involuntary squeak.

"Did you find something?" asked Imogen, smiling at a couple who were headed out the door.

"Yes!" Ophelia whispered. "There's a Robert Sugden who checked in three weeks ago. Paid for the best suite in advance for a full month."

"Sugden?" Imogen risked a glance at the register. "That's a coincidence. It could be someone related to the Sugdens in Saffron Weald."

"And look at these expenditures! He's ordered a bottle of wine every night as well as charged expensive meals in the restaurant to his room." Ophelia's finger traced down the itemized bill.

"Someone's coming!" Imogen warned, angling herself to better block the desk as Ophelia quickly flipped the register closed and ran around to the customer's side of the desk.

Speaking more loudly than usual, Pierre retraced his steps to the lobby with the receptionist in tow as the twins casually leaned on the desk.

"I'm extremely impressed with the menu," they heard him say.

The young woman giggled. "Do you want to book a stay then?"

Pierre glanced at his watch. "The delicious scent of that food 'as made me rather 'ungry. I think I'll sample a meal before making a booking."

The girl's smile slipped. "As you wish."

As Pierre stepped away, the young woman thanked the twins for watching the reception. "Are you registered?"

"No, we had heard good things about the place and wanted to have a look. But you're busy." Another couple had drawn close and asked for their key. The twins stepped back and with Pierre, disappeared into the flow of people crossing the entry.

"Ladies, what do you say to an early dinner?"

After savoring an appetizing meal, and ordering coffee and dessert, Ophelia's mind returned to their current mysteries.

"Regarding your elephant clock and the mysterious miniature key, has our trap worked yet?"

"No, but I 'ave changed the door locks, front and back. If the person who placed the key in the clock broke in to my shop, they will 'ave a much 'arder time now. Plus, I put barrel bolts at the top of the doors, so even if they are able to overcome the new locks, they still can't get in—when I'm in bed, at least. Obviously, I cannot be in the store every minute of every day. And even though that valuable ring was stolen, it does not seem enough to warrant 'iring a security guard for when I'm not there."

A waiter appeared to remove their plates and asked if they needed more coffee. They all declined.

As he departed, Ophelia asked, "How much was that ring worth?"

Pierre quirked a brow. "£100."

"Phew! That seems a lot of money to lose. Have you contacted the police?"

"Certainly. I filed a report with Constable 'Argrove. But while you were engaged with our interesting friend Henry, I 'ad a good look around 'is pawn shop. I did not see my ring. But I think it would be wise to pay a visit to all the pawnbrokers in the area."

"It's the violation of your privacy that bothers me most," said Ophelia taking his hand across the table. "Your home is your sanctum sanctorum."

"What about a security dog who's paid in bones?" asked

Imogen with a twinkle in her eye. "For when you can't be in the store, I mean?"

Ophelia squeezed Pierre's hand. "Imogen, that's brilliant. No one will try to break in when they hear Tiger's deep bark."

"Well ... " He made the typically French hunch with his shoulders.

Ophelia pushed her palms together as if in prayer. "Just until the thief is uncovered."

The sound of china clinking and people chatting, filled the silence as Pierre considered.

"Alright," he finally said. "'E's a good boy and I, as you say, can fetch 'im a bone from *Cleaver's* to keep 'im busy. We shall 'ave to coordinate our calendars."

"I don't suppose you're any further along in discovering what the key is for?"

"No. I know it is *not* a bank deposit key. 'Owever, when Henry gave you the key to the trunk, it did make me wonder if it could be the key to a private keepsake box, though it is much more ornate than the typical ones."

Ophelia's mind again wandered to the special box she kept under her own bed. "That is certainly a possibility, but as you pointed out when we found it, the real mystery is how the key ended up in the clock in the first place. I assume you took the clock apart when you first bought it?"

"Certainement. I took it all to pieces, cleaning every element before putting it back together again. The key, it was not there."

The couple seated at the next table, paid their bill and left. Ophelia watched them as she thought about what Pierre had said. "So, it was placed in the clock sometime between when you first displayed it in your shop and taking it up to your apartment."

Pierre stroked the neat beard on his chin. "And that was a relatively short time—a matter of days. But the timing does coincide with when the two larger crowds came in."

"Did any of them buy anything? Perhaps you recorded their names?" asked Imogen.

"Oh, yes. I made a lot of sales but I merely write receipts for the items purchased, I do not take the names and addresses of the purchasers. The only time I would, is if we need to deliver an item or if the customer cannot pay for the item in full. Though, it's too bad, because if I 'ad, I could contact them to ask about the other members of the group and obtain their names and addresses."

"Do you remember anything about them? Did they have a group name?"

"Unfortunately, I don't recall. But no matter. The police will keep looking for the groups because of the theft, at least for a while."

"What did you think of *Humble Henry*? He's quite a character, isn't he? Honestly, he still scares the life out of me," admitted Imogen. "You should have seen Ophelia the first time. She was fearless and bartered with the demon mercilessly."

"I can well imagine." Pierre laughed and several women turned to look.

"Getting back to our current problem. It is clear we don't really know Kitty Fairfax at all. Furthermore, we *do* know the name of the rogue who scared her the night of the first rehearsal. Jack Scroggins. And we also have proof he is still in the vicinity."

"I suppose you 'ave considered the possibility that Fairfax is not 'er real name?" asked Pierre.

"Ever since hearing about the fire and learning that she is not from Birmingham, I have wondered if that is her real name." She snapped her fingers. "I've had a brain wave! Since we're in Parkford, we should go to the county library and search the national papers for deadly fires in Liverpool in the last five years." She glanced at her watch. "They're open for another hour and a half."

"With three of us looking, we might get lucky," agreed Imogen.

Pierre raised his hand for the bill.

"And when we get home, I want to ask Molly and Ed about this Robert Sugden. A Sugden being listed in the hotel register is more than chance, if you ask me."

The Parkford County library was housed in a Victorian edifice that seemed designed to intimidate rather than welcome. Inside, the air hung heavy with the musty perfume of old paper and furniture polish. The two-story space was eerily quiet except for the occasional scrape of chair legs against wooden floors and the rustle of turning pages.

All around them, other patrons bent over desks like medieval scribes, making careful notes from leather-bound volumes. The late afternoon light filtered through tall windows, creating pools of dusty sunshine on the worn wooden tables.

They converged on a severe looking librarian sorting cards and replacing them in books. By common consent, they let Pierre take the lead again.

"Excuse me."

The iron woman's head snapped up, her eyes taking in the handsome Frenchman. She touched the hair at her neck.

"How may I help you, sir?"

"May I just say how lovely you look today." The twins exchanged a glance.

The stern expression slipped away from the librarian's face like butter off hot bread. "Why thank you."

"We're interested in researching the last several years of national newspapers."

From the woman's expression, this was an unusual request. She pointed to a door on the left that said 'Periodicals'.

"You should find everything you need in that office."

Pierre doffed his hat and bowed, and the officious woman was reduced to mush. "'Ow can I ever thank you?"

They ambled over to the door and Ophelia looked back to see the lady's eyes still on Pierre, a hand to her chest.

A tall, thin man in gold spectacles sat at the information desk in the periodicals space and once they had made their request, he directed them to the long tables.

He reappeared with a trolley on wheels and eight large boxes. "Just a reminder that we close at five o'clock."

Imogen stared wide-eyed. *"Hot crumpets!* How are we ever going to get through them?"

Ophelia took off her coat and rolled up her sleeves. "One newspaper at a time, ducky. Now, Kitty has been in the area since August of last year, so we can ignore anything after that."

Pierre placed his hat on the table. "A fire that killed several people would have made the first or second page of a newspaper so no need to look through the whole paper."

Ophelia opened the first box and discarded it. "These are too recent." She opened the next box and pulled out a pile. "I doubt it happened in July as it would take time to mourn and then find a job."

"Let's start with March of last year then," suggested Imogen.

After an hour of research, they had come up with nothing but eye ache.

Pierre slumped back in his chair. "That's January to March of last year and the whole of the year before that."

"Let's get cracking on 1926."

"I'm going to take a quick look in April to June of last year, while you do that," said Imogen pushing hair out of her eyes that had disengaged from her bun. "Challenge our assumptions."

Another twenty minutes passed, and the librarian gave them the side eye.

"Bingo!" shouted Imogen then immediately regretted it. "Sorry." She dropped her voice and pushed the paper to the middle of the table pointing to the bottom of the front page.

TRAGIC FIRE CLAIMS FAMILY IN BILLINGS, LANCASHIRE, screamed the headline. If the famous Lady Harcourt had not died, the story would have been *above* the fold.

In the early hours of Tuesday morning, a devastating fire swept through 36 North Street, Billings, near Liverpool, leaving one survivor and claiming the lives of almost an entire family. The blaze, which began in the sitting room, tore through the terraced house with alarming speed.

The sole survivor, Miss Lucy Katherine Ellis, 22, escaped the inferno but sustained severe burns to her upper arm when struck by a falling beam during her desperate attempt to reach other family members. Miss Ellis was conveyed to Liverpool East Hospital where she was treated and later released. When questioned by authorities, the young woman appeared severely shocked and could offer no explanation for the fire's origin.

The Liverpool Fire Brigade fought valiantly to contain the blaze, successfully preventing its spread to adjacent properties, though neighboring houses suffered considerable smoke damage. In an unfortunate addition to the tragedy, a neighbor's cat perished in the disaster.

Fire Chief, William Morton, described the conflagration as "the most severe domestic fire to strike the Liverpool region in three decades." He added that an investigation into the cause is ongoing.

The Ellis family were well-known in the Billings district, having had ancestors who lived in the village for over two hundred years.

"Well, I never!" declared Imogen. "How horrible. Losing her whole family, like that. No wonder she wanted to start all over again."

Ophelia heaved a great sigh. "I know you are going to hate me for saying this and I hardly dare draw this conclusion, but what if Kitty set the fire?"

"You think—no! She's the victim here," said Imogen in Kitty's defense.

"What do you think, Pierre?" asked Ophelia.

Pierre tapped the newspaper article. "As investigators, we must review the facts with no emotion. Pretend we don't know the girl. What would you think about the fire chief's last comment coupled with Kitty's flight to Meadowshire and the name change?"

Imogen's whole frame sagged. *"Blasted buttons!* If I look at it that way, it's awfully fishy."

"The question is," Ophelia said carefully, "if Kitty set the fire, what was her motive?"

"Or was it truly an accident?" Imogen touched the newspaper

article gently. "Sometimes terrible things just happen."

Pierre gathered their coats. "There's only one way to find out."

"You mean confront her?" Imogen's voice wavered. "After what happened to Farmer Jones, is that a good idea?"

"It doesn't have to be an ambush," Ophelia said. "We can simply invite her to tea and give her the chance to tell her story. After all, she's either a victim who needs our help…"

"Or a cold-blooded murderer who's killed before," Imogen finished grimly. "And one who might not have any qualms about killing again."

CHAPTER 14

Family Sins

E d Sugden rubbed his chubby hands together. "What can I do for you, Miss Harrington?"

"I'm in the mood for lemon drops. I'll take a quarter of a pound, please." She glanced around the store. The Sugdens had done a really good job of redecorating, but she was here under a false premise, to upset the apple cart.

Ed tipped the large glass container of lemon drops into the scales. "It's a little under. Is that ok?"

Ophelia appreciated it when shopkeepers did not try to take advantage of their customers by putting too much on the scales. "Perfect."

"How are you and your family taking the untimely passing of Farmer Jones?" she asked as Ed slid the sweets into a paper bag. It had been three days since the murder and not one article had reached the papers. The inspector must be keeping a tight lid on things since the fatality was accidental. "It's not every day you witness someone die right in front of you."

"You can say that again! We came down to Meadowshire for a bit of quiet. Poor lad. I hear it was his heart."

Ophelia praised heaven that Mildred had not got hold of the truth yet. If she had, the entire village would be wagging their tongues like a pack of thirsty dogs.

"Umm," she replied non-committally. "Were things bad in Manchester?"

The pleasant expression fled from Ed's face. "Why do you ask?"

She allowed a softness to creep into her reply. "You just said you came down here for some quiet."

The confectioner's shoulders relaxed. "Oh, that. It's just a figure of speech. You know." He handed her the bag.

"How does Saffron Weald compare to Manchester?" She popped a lemon drop in her mouth and dropped the bag into her basket.

"Do you know Manchester?" Was that fear in his eyes?

"No. Not at all. Our orchestra played there once, but it was a one-night-only performance and we left early the next morning."

"Right. Violin innit?"

"Yes. I recently retired."

"My Molly, she's mad for classical music." He stopped short of saying he hated it, but it was inferred.

"How are your boys settling in? It's such a hard age to move."

"They miss their friends, but we told them what a good opportunity this was and they were both on board."

"Did I hear they play cricket? There's a county team, you know. They could try out when the weather gets better."

"I think someone did mention it, yes." She got the impression he was ready for her to leave.

"And do you have family still in Manchester?"

He could not suppress a sigh. "Uh, just some cousins. Both our parents have passed on."

She had to know if the person listed as a guest at *The Lion* was any relation. She took a chance. "Any here in Meadowshire?"

Ed's expression changed from mildly wary to downright leery. "No."

"It's just that I was in Parkford yesterday and I ran into Robert."

Horror bloomed across Ed's features like ink in water, his mouth working silently as he gripped the edge of the counter so hard his knuckles turned white.

"Y-you met my b-brother?"

Bingo!

"Yes, Robert, or does he go by Bobby?"

His face broke out in a sweat. "B-Bob. Just Bob."

"I was so surprised since neither you nor Molly had mentioned him."

"I'm as surprised as you, Miss Harrington. Wait till I tell Molly." He sounded about as enthusiastic as someone identifying a body at the morgue. She had a feeling she was witnessing a man discovering that his carefully constructed new life was about to unravel. She felt awful.

Ophelia watched Ed struggle to regain his composure, noting how his hands trembled as he pretended to reorganize the display of penny caramels.

"Funny thing is," she continued casually, "he seemed to be doing quite well for himself at *The Lion.* Very well indeed."

Ed's hand knocked against the glass jar, sending it wobbling dangerously close to the edge. Molly appeared from the back room just in time to steady it.

"Everything alright, luv?" she asked, her eyes darting between her husband's ashen features and Ophelia's carefully neutral expression, the tension between them charging the air like the moments before lightning strikes.

"Miss Harrington, here, was just telling me she ran into B-Bob in Parkford," Ed managed, his throttled voice barely above a whisper.

The measuring scoop Molly had been holding, clattered to the floor, the sound sharp as a gunshot in the sudden silence. "Bob? Here?" Her voice had risen an octave. "But that's not ... he couldn't be..."

"At *The Lion Hotel*," Ophelia added, taking no pleasure in watching as the pleasant couple exchanged looks of pure panic. "Staying in the best suite, I understand. Quite the gentleman of leisure."

"There must be some mistake," Molly said quickly. "Bob's not ... that is, he couldn't possibly..." She stopped, seemingly unable to finish any of her sentences.

"I seem to have brought you bad news," Ophelia said slowly. "I didn't mean any harm. I was just in Parkford ..." Since her suspicions had been confirmed, she had no desire to torture the distraught couple any further, but she *was* itching to know exactly *what* the problem with Bob was and if it could be a motive for trying to kill his sister-in-law.

Suddenly, Molly whipped around the counter and flipped the sign on the door to 'closed'. "Won't you stay for a cuppa?" Her face was contorted with anguish.

It was an unexpected invitation that Ophelia found she could not refuse. "If you're sure?"

Molly took Ed's trembling hand in hers. "I'm sure. I've already got the kettle boiled. Ed, take our guest into the sitting room."

Ed did as he was told but seemed extremely unhappy about it.

"I don't want to intrude," said Ophelia, though it was far from the truth since she *was* investigating a murder.

Ed showed her to a floral armchair and situated himself on a blue settee but stared at the door awaiting his wife's return. She was not long and offered Ophelia a cup and saucer, placing a sugar bowl on the coffee table. Ophelia could not help noticing she brought nothing for herself and Ed.

"You're probably wondering what's the matter?" Molly began, trying but failing to smile. "We were hoping we'd never have to tell this tale, or certainly not this soon." She gripped Ed's hand. "But you and your sister have been so welcoming, and we've heard about some of the things you've done for this village so, I think perhaps you deserve to know the truth."

Ophelia said not a word.

Molly squeezed her husband's hand. Ed's eyes began to shine.

"It's a fact of life that you can't choose your family," she began. Ed nodded.

"Though sometimes you wish you could," she sighed. "Ed's

brother Robert, Bob, is a bad'un. He was a naughty little boy, a troublemaker in his youth, and a criminal before he became an adult. I'm not exaggerating when I say he put Ed's mother in an early grave."

Ed nodded morosely again.

Molly continued. "Ten years ago in 1919, right after the war ended, Bob and his motely crew of pals decided to rob a bank."

Ophelia could not suppress her shock. "A bank?" Her mind sprang forward. Bob Sugden must be living large off the ill-gotten funds from the robbery.

"They managed to get away with a lot of money which they stashed somewhere." Molly drew a hand under her nose. "But they all got drunk while celebrating and one of the blokes boasted about what they'd done. Stupid, because the robbery had been front page news. They were all arrested and sent to prison for ten years. But the police never found the money."

"Blazing bagpipes!" said Ophelia, lost for words.

"Guilt by association is a real thing, let me tell you. People would whisper behind our backs and walk out of shops when we entered. We even stopped getting invitations. It nigh on broke my heart. But as the boys grew up, they got old enough to see that we were being shunned and understood the nasty rumors. We'd kept it from them, you see. And with Bob's release date right around the corner we decided we needed to leave Manchester behind and start a new life. For the boys mostly. *I* could handle the cold shoulders, but I didn't want that for Mark and David."

Ophelia put her cup on the table and folded her hands on her lap. "And now I've just told you that Bob is here, in Meadowshire and shattered your peace. I'm *so* sorry."

"I don't know how he found us. We didn't tell anyone we were leaving, just upped and left one night. And by the sounds of it, he's retrieved the stolen cash."

"I don't want to leave again," groaned Ed. "I like it here and the boys will settle in soon."

Ophelia hated what she had to do next. "Look, we found a

book of matches from *The Lion* on the stage—"

"You mean Bob was here in Saffron Weald?"

"Slow down. Let's not give in to hysteria. I told a bit of a fib about meeting him. The truth is, we took the matches we found on the stage after the murder, to the hotel. They confirmed that it is this year's branding on the cover. Then, I may have peeked in the register while we distracted the receptionist and found your brother's name in the ledger. But it does not necessarily follow that the matches were his and prove his presence in Saffron Weald."

"Bit of a coincidence, though, innit?" Bob's round face was pinched with fear.

"It is," Ophelia conceded, "and there's another piece of troubling news, I'm afraid. We didn't want to cause alarm the night of the incident, but Nicholas Jones did not die of a heart attack. He was poisoned."

Ed's large frame lolled sideways on the sofa and Ophelia thought he might pass out. Molly began fanning him with a magazine.

"He's gone from robbery to murder," moaned Ed, his cheek smooshed into the couch.

"Now, now. Let's not jump to conclusions," warned Ophelia. "But I must also tell you that the wrong person was murdered."

Ed moaned. "Ahh! It goes from bad to worse."

"Wrong person?" asked Molly. "Who was it supposed to be?"

Ophelia pursed her lips. "One of you leading ladies."

This snapped Ed out of his fugue. "He tried to kill my Molly?"

"First of all, there are *four* leading ladies," Ophelia pointed out. "The poison was put in one of the wineglass props. At this point, we don't know who the intended target was. All we do know is that Farmer Jones drank the poison by accident."

"Bob blames me for turning you against him," murmured Molly looking like she'd seen a ghost. "I'll bet that poison was intended for me. Bob's not big on forgiveness."

"It wasn't you that turned me against Bob! It was him! That violent streak. Giving my mother that heart attack," cried Ed.

"He might not see it that way," Molly choked out.

"Knowing what you've told me, I strongly suggest you tell Inspector Southam all this. That way he can offer you protection from your brother."

"And you found the matches on the stage, you say? Oh, Ed. He's been watching us this whole time. The play, the rehearsals, everything. He's been here all along."

Ed slumped forward, face in his hands. "He's playing games with us, luv. We'll have to leave again."

A tremendous crash from downstairs in the shop, scared them all half to death. Molly's shaky hands flew to her mouth, sending Ophelia's teacup spinning across the carpet. Through the sitting room door came the ominous sound of breaking glass.

"Sorry, mam!"

Relief flooded Molly's features. "It's just David and Mark. Home from school."

"David knocked over a jar!" shouted Mark up the stairs.

"I've never been so glad that something is just broken," gasped Molly.

Ophelia retrieved the cup and gathered her things. "Well, I'll leave you now. You have a lot to tell the boys and you should call the inspector as soon as possible."

Ophelia glanced over her shoulder as she left the *Jolly Lolly*. Bob Sugden must be some tyrant to cause that much fear in his own family.

CHAPTER 15

The Spider and the Fly

R elaxing in front of a roaring fire in the Badger's Hollow lounge, Kitty sipped tea and ate their mother's famous cake. Like spiders spinning a silken trap, the twins had invited the young teacher into their parlor, and Imogen's guilt grew as she watched their unsuspecting guest make herself comfortable. Tiger had decided Kitty was his new best friend and nudged up tight against her legs, head on her lap, making moon eyes. Every now and then, he would heave a dramatic sigh of contentment, his tail thumping softly against the rug whenever she found a particularly pleasing place to scratch.

The sitting room, with its massive inglenook fireplace, formed the entertaining part of the house, just as it had in the Elizabethan times when the cottage was built. Polished oak beams, darkened by age and woodsmoke, crossed the ceiling like ancient branches, while the duchess's furniture – rescued from obscurity by Pierre's keen eye – lent an air of faded elegance to the room. A delicate French settee, its damask upholstery carefully restored, faced the fireplace where gentle flames danced behind the wrought iron guard.

"Let me know if Tiger is bothering you," said Imogen.

"Not at all." Kitty ran an experienced hand across his head

finding the sweet spot behind his ears that made his back leg twitch. She spoke in the Brummie accent they now knew was fake. "We had dogs growing up. I luv 'em."

Tiger rolled his head to press his wet nose into her palm, as if sensing her upcoming need for comfort. When she paused in her petting to take a sip of tea, he shoved her palm with his muzzle, brown eyes pleading for more attention. The twins exchanged glances. Tiger was usually more reserved with strangers, yet here he was, behaving like a pampered lapdog.

Though everything in their investigation now pointed to Bob Sugden targeting his sister-in-law Molly with the poison, something about this tidy conclusion nagged at them both. The Sugdens had gone straight to the police after Ophelia's visit, telling them everything.

The inspector acted without delay and brought Bob in for questioning. Despite admitting to lurking around Saffron Weald, Bob claimed he only wanted to reconcile with his brother. More importantly, he had an iron-clad alibi for the night of the dress rehearsal – he'd been buying rounds at the *Fatted Calf* in Parkford, witnessed by fifty people.

Inspector Southam seemed satisfied. He was a lot more interested in Bob's suspicious wealth than in placing him on the list of suspects for the murder. But the twins kept this solution to the crime on the back burner. They had learned that alibis, even seemingly solid ones, could crumble under closer scrutiny.

As the next potential poisoning victim on the list, they felt it their duty to inform Kitty that she might be in danger. At the same time, they would confess that they knew she had lied about her past. But it tugged at Imogen's heart that they were about to shatter Kitty's peace of mind.

"I'm sure you know by now that Farmer Jones was not the intended victim of the poisoning," began Ophelia.

Kitty turned wide, green eyes on her. "I did hear that. What a terrible mistake."

"Have you given any thought to who might have been the target of the poisoner?" asked Ophelia.

Kitty's mouth pulled down in a shrug. "I haven't. I just feel terrible for the Jones family."

Imogen crossed her hands on her lap. "But you know the poison was found in the wineglass prop?"

"Yes. I remember Alice getting her dress wet—" Kitty stopped sharp. "Are you saying the poison was meant for one of us?"

"There's no way around it, Kitty. No one else was supposed to drink from those glasses. Do you remember if the glass in front of you was empty?"

Paralyzed by fear, Kitty stayed quiet. Tiger tipped his head and put a paw on her knee.

"Kitty dear, can you remember where that wineglass was?"

The dog made a soft whining sound as if to encourage the girl.

She spoke quietly. "Mine was empty. The glasses were brought on by the women's chorus. Molly rearranged them, then Judith slid them directly in front of each of us for the scene. She's particular about things like that. I-I can't remember where the full glass was. Perhaps by Celina? They were supposed to be empty, of course, so we were all confused, but we were in rehearsal mode, so it was a quick thought and we moved on." Something clicked. "Y-you think it was meant for me?"

Imogen asked quietly, "Do you have any reason to believe someone would want to hurt you?"

Eyes fixed on her clasped hands, Kitty mumbled, "No."

"Is that entirely true, ducky? I'm afraid we've done a little investigating and we know about the fire."

Fear shadowed Kitty's eyes. "You do?"

"Yes, and we also know that you have not been entirely honest with the good people of Saffron Weald."

Kitty's whole frame wilted. "I can explain." She said the last phrase in her native Liverpudlian accent.

"We were hoping you would, lovey."

The room was silent except for the popping of the fire. Kitty squirmed as if summoning the strength to reveal the truth. She sighed. "As you must know, I'm from Liverpool not Birmingham. I was running away from my old life and wanted a fresh start.

And I'm good at accents.

"I *was* seeing a young man there and I *did* go to teacher training college, and I *was* the first in my family to get a college education. Those things are all true." Her expression begged for their understanding. "My father had a tannery on the edge of the village. He made a decent living and we lived in a terraced house in the middle of the village. He insisted that all his children go to school and learn to read. He'd say the world was changing and skills like his would die out." Kitty shifted in her chair, nervously pulling at her skirt. "I had a friend, a boy who lived next door, and as children we were inseparable. But as we got older, he was influenced by a gang operating in our area. He began stealing things and I distanced myself." She reached out to touch Tiger's ears as if they could give her the confidence to continue. "Just after my fourteenth birthday, he came to me and said he was done with all that. He wanted me to be his girl and knew I didn't approve of his friends. Like an idiot, I believed him and we started courting. We had to do it in secret because my dad knew all about his bad behavior and did not approve." A hand strayed to her wild hair and she began to curl a strand around her finger. "When my teacher recommended me for teacher training, my dad was that proud. He even paid for my education. Jack, the boy, begged me not to go. He even proposed. But I couldn't disappoint my dad, and though I didn't admit as much to Jack, I craved knowledge. I was sent to be a pupil teacher on the other side of Liverpool and attend the training college there.

"While I was gone, he fell back in with the gang, though I didn't know it at the time, and he managed to keep it from me during the summers. He left school at fifteen to go to work and help support his family.

"I finished my training after two years and came home to get a job at my old school and re-ignite my relationship with Jack. But this time I could tell he was different. Darker. Moody. One of my old classmates told me he and the gang had beaten up an old lady and stolen her purse.

"I confronted Jack and he got defensive. Asked me who was

telling lies about him. The light had gone out of him, you know? He proposed again and demanded that I give up my job to be a proper wife. I refused." She wiped her cheek. "That night I woke up to the smell of smoke. I bolted down the stairs and found the front room glowing orange through the gap under the door. The heat hit me like a wall when I opened it. The sofa was on fire. I tried to put it out but before I could smother it, the flames caught the curtains. They went up like paper, sending sparks floating up to the ceiling. I dashed out of the room and closed the door, hoping to stop its progress, but the blaze burned through the ceiling and into the bedrooms above. I could hear it roaring, eating through the floorboards. Smoke was everywhere by then – thick, choking clouds that made my eyes stream and my lungs burn. I could hear a terrible creaking sound as the house's bones began to give way." She stared into the hearth, not seeing anything. "I put my nightdress to my mouth and attempted to barrel up the stairs to warn my family but there was a wall of flames that beat me back. I called for them through the cloth. The smoke was so dense, I couldn't see the next step, and I could feel the heat pushing me back. I panicked when I heard my mother cry out, and my father shouting something I couldn't make out. My heart about broke when I heard the children's cries. Overcome with fear at the sound of their voices, I struggled to go up the stairs again but the heat was so intense and I couldn't breathe." Sobbing now, Kitty could hardly speak.

"Then came the most horrible noise – the crack and groan of the timber giving way. The last thing I remember was the banister coming down, bringing with it a shower of burning hot debris. It hit my arm and the pain was like nothing I'd ever felt before. Everything after that is a blur."

Hence the desire for long sleeves!

The twins let Kitty weep, waiting until she was ready to continue. She pulled a handkerchief from her sleeve, wiping her nose and eyes, trying to catch her breath.

"When I came to, I was lying on the wet cobbles, watching my whole world burned to ash."

Imogen offered her a clean handkerchief and Tiger licked her knees.

"I stayed with a friend for a while after the funerals, hardly leaving the house. Jack came by several times, but I wouldn't see him." She raised her head, her eyes rimmed with grief. "You see, I believe he set the fire because I rebuffed him."

"*Hot crumpets!*" cried Imogen. "Was he so cruel?"

"Not in the old days. But he had changed. I don't think he meant the fire to kill anyone. I think it got out of control too quickly."

"Did the police conduct an investigation?" asked Ophelia.

"They did but there were no witnesses, so the official report said it was an accident. I didn't have the energy to oppose it."

Ophelia slid forward in her chair and took Kitty's hand. "Oh, my dear, this is truly tragic."

"When I resurfaced, I just wanted to get away, but I didn't want anyone to know about my history, so I reinvented myself. My real name is Lucy Katherine Ellis. My mother called me Kitty."

The whole room seemed to weep for the battered girl before them.

Imogen pursed her lips. "Then I feel simply horrid that we have brought you the bad news that *you* could have been the target, here in Saffron Weald."

"I'm just never going to be shot of him, am I?" The tears toppled over her lower lids and down her cheeks, splashing onto her fingers.

"Is Jack the man I saw you with?" asked Imogen.

Kitty sucked in air. "It was. I'm so sorry I had to lie to you, Miss Harrington. I was so shaken that he found me. I still don't know how."

"What did you say to him?"

"I told him to leave me alone and go home, that I had a new life now, one that did not include him."

A piece of wood snapped in the grate, distracting them all for a moment.

"What did he say?" asked Imogen.

"He gripped me by the arm. I flinched. It was the arm that got burned and I told him so. That made him shrink back as if I'd slapped him. He swore he had not set the fire, but his heart wasn't in the denial and I didn't believe him. That's when you came out, Mrs. Pettigrew, and he sped off."

"Does this Jack smoke Woodbine cigarettes?" asked Imogen.

Kitty closed her eyes. "He does."

"I found a pile of them by the oak tree. He'd been waiting for some time. Worse, we found one on the stage."

Kitty's head jerked up.

"Have you seen him since?" asked Ophelia.

"No. I assumed he'd gone back to Liverpool."

"I'd be careful with that assumption, ducky. We found a gentleman's trunk at a pawnshop in Parkford yesterday. It had Jack Scroggin's belongings inside and letters from you."

She seemed resigned. "He's still here."

"He is," said Ophelia. "And it might just be Jack who put poison in your glass!"

CHAPTER 16

Whispers and Warnings

Before Kitty left, they put through a call to Inspector Southam and she gave him a briefer version of her story. He promised to be on the lookout for Jack and to bring him in for questioning and admonished her to stay with someone for a few days as a precaution. She immediately contacted another teacher in Willowbrook and made the necessary arrangements.

After Kitty left, Imogen asked Ophelia, "What do you make of it all?"

The fire still crackled in the grate, but it no longer seemed comforting. Instead, it brought to mind Kitty's tragic story.

"I'd say we've found another worthy candidate for the murderer."

Imogen gathered up the tea things. "Some people get dealt such a bad hand in life, don't you think? We've been so fortunate."

"That was one of the first realizations I had as an adult; life is unfair. I hope Kitty won't lose her job when it comes out that she wasn't totally honest on her application."

"I don't know the headmistress in Willowbrook, but I'm going to assume she's a reasonable woman who will understand the tight corner Kitty was facing. Personally, I feel nothing but compassion for the poor girl. I can't imagine losing your whole family in one fell swoop. It would crush me."

"It's a horrible way to die, that's for certain." Ophelia stirred the fire with a poker. "In order to dot all our 'i's and 't's, we should interview the two other leading ladies. If this has taught us anything, it's that people like to keep their skeletons under lock and key."

"We can start with Celina." Imogen raised a book from the side table by her chair. "I need to take this back to the library, anyway."

The compact Saffron Weald library, built in the same Elizabethan style as the rest of the village, began life as a small school. The librarian, Celina, was quite young but extremely competent. A line of people faced her desk, ready to check out books. The twins joined the back of the line behind Harriet Cleaver, the butcher's wife.

"Hello." Harriet dropped her voice, the tone conspiratorial. "I heard about the tragedy at the dress rehearsal the other night. Atrocious! What is the world coming to?"

Though the police had made a concerted effort to keep the truth under wraps to prevent a panic, word that Farmer Jones's death was no accident had evidently begun to spread through the village. Was it also common knowledge that Farmer Jones was not the intended victim?

Ophelia crossed her arms. "The war changed the world in my opinion. People don't value human life like they used to."

"I agree," said Harriet. "Harold and I said the same thing when we heard about Farmer Jones. Who has Nicholas ever hurt?" She moved closer. "Are you two looking into it?"

Ophelia nodded. "Unofficially, yes."

"Found any clues?" Harriet clasped her handbag to her chest as if it were a shield.

"Some. But it's early days," explained Ophelia, indicating that the queue had moved.

Harriet shuffled forward. "Well, you two always seem to be one step ahead of the police."

"Next!" called Celina, and Harriet swirled round, handing the librarian her book.

"I'd say the village grapevine has not yet uncovered the fact that the wrong person was murdered," whispered Imogen.

Ophelia tutted. "It's only a matter of time."

Harriet bid the twins good day and they stepped up to the desk.

Imogen directed her gaze at Celina. "Can we have a word?"

This was not the first time the twins had approached Celina at work while investigating a mystery, and she recognized their tone. Looking beyond them, she saw there was only one other person in line.

"Let me check them out and I'll meet you in my office."

Under the tenure of the former librarian, the walls of the glorified cupboard had been covered with cat pictures. Now, those same small walls held a picture of the Bodleian Libraries at Oxford University and a pen and ink portrait of Shakespeare.

They each cast an eye over the only chair on the patron side of the desk.

"You can sit." Ophelia gestured to the chair.

Celina rushed in and closed the door. "Is this about Farmer Jones?"

"It is. Have the police talked to you?"

"Of course. We were all interviewed that night."

Imogen clasped her hands. "I meant since then?"

Celina dropped into her chair, jaw taut, hands pulling at her collar. "Why should they? I didn't see anything. I already told them."

"There's been a ... development." Ophelia held Celina's gaze.

Shoulders hunched as if warding off a blow, Celina asked, "What is it?" The words came out slowly, almost as a question but also as a statement of disbelief.

"I'm afraid you should know we have good reason to believe Nicholas Jones was killed by accident. He took a swig of the liquid in the prop wineglass." Ophelia let the sentence hang in the air between them.

Celina was a bright girl and she sensed their meaning immediately. "It was destined for one of us." Grabbing her throat, she searched Ophelia's face. "You think it was meant for *me*?"

"Would anyone have a reason to kill you?"

Celina deflated, scratching an eyebrow with resignation. "Normally, I would say no, but I received a hate letter right after Christmas. Somehow, one of the relatives of the man my aunt killed over the patent of the rubber boot lining, found out I worked here and sent me a note claiming I owed them money." Her fingers trembled as she swept her hair behind her ear. "I found it rather unsettling, but I didn't really take it seriously. Are you saying I should?"

The twins had seen the aftermath of her aunt's crimes firsthand – murders that tried to cover up her grandfather's sin. They should have guessed those ripples might eventually reach Celina.

"How threatening was the letter?"

"Pretty nasty." She brought her hand up to cover her mouth. "I took it straight to Constable Hargrove. He contacted the constabulary in the town of origin, according to the postmark. They knew exactly who it was and warned the writer they were committing extortion and would be prosecuted if they continued to contact me. I haven't heard anything since."

"Well, it's not nothing," sighed Ophelia.

"But you're not the only one of the leading ladies to have cause for concern," added Imogen. "Two of the others believe *they* could have been the intended target, but until we know for certain who the killer meant to poison, you'll need to take some safety measures, Celina."

The librarian eyed the coffee cup on her desk with suspicion. "You're suggesting that because the killer failed to kill the right person they might try again?"

Imogen sliced the air with her hand. "I know it sounds

alarming but if you stay alert, I see no need to fear. Is there someone you could stay with since you live alone?"

Celina's face fell. "Good heavens! You think it's that serious?" She cast her eyes about the tiny room. "I suppose I could stay with my mother in Parkford. I'll have to close the library."

Ophelia's expression was grim. "Good idea. It's a small price to pay until we find out who the murderer is."

Celina began throwing things in a large blue handbag. "You don't have to tell me twice!"

The twins still needed to interview Judith Rutherford, the final leading lady, but school was still in session. Ophelia suggested they pass the remaining forty minutes at *Thyme For Tea* rather than go home.

The usual cheerful bustle of Saffron Weald had dimmed since Farmer Jones' death. The streets, normally alive with gossip and laughter, held only hushed conversations full of speculations about strangers, and worried glances. The shadow of murder had fallen across their peaceful village once again, and not even the bright spring sunshine could quite dispel it.

"Ladies!" Matilda's tone was lacking its usual mother-hen enthusiasm "I just got in some fresh rock cakes from Puddingfield's. They're still hot!"

The sweet smell of the cakes confirmed her words. "Then we'll take one each," said Imogen.

Matilda hurried off, an anxious frown carving a channel into her forehead.

Prudence Cresswell, the vicar's wife, was sitting with Patricia Snodgrass, but by the looks of it, they were getting ready to leave. The twins took the table next to them.

"Any news?" asked Prudence, her long nose quivering.

"Nothing concrete that we feel at liberty to share," explained Imogen, pulling her chair closer to the crochet-topped table.

"But that means you *have* made progress," said Patricia, eyes flaming with curiosity. "Poor Elizabeth Jones is devastated. They have no sons, you know. How is she supposed to run the farm by herself?"

"The vicar and I were talking, and we think it must have been a horrible accident. Perhaps someone didn't know the liquid in that bottle was poison and put it in the glass as a joke."

Well, you're right about the accident.

"That's one theory." Ophelia delivered her sweetest smile.

Patricia pulled on her gloves. "Have the police arrested anyone? There's been very little about it in the papers."

Imogen laid her own gloves on the tablecloth. "No arrests as far as we know, but there are several people of interest."

"I always feel so exposed before the killer is found," exclaimed Patricia. "Living alone, one imagines every noise to be the murderer trying to get into the house."

"I can well imagine," said Ophelia who had lived alone for most of her adult life.

"I've been walking the children to school," added Prudence.

"It's good to know you're looking into it." Patricia snapped her handbag closed. "The police seem a little ... slow."

"You have to remember that this will not be the only case that has landed in their laps," said Imogen, defending the local constabulary. "We're only too happy to help."

Matilda returned with their tea and cakes as Prudence and Patricia said their goodbyes. Once they left, Matilda pulled a seat up to the twins' table.

"I had to get the doctor to give me something to calm my nerves." She touched the curls at the side of her face with trembling fingers. "I'm too old for all this intrigue."

"It *is* distressing," agreed Ophelia.

"I couldn't sleep," she continued as if Ophelia had not said a word. "I lay awake clutching the covers and staring at the ceiling, frightened out of my wits at every sound."

"Have you thought about when we *will* put on the show?" Imogen pulled the sugar bowl toward her.

Matilda looked at Imogen as if she were stupid. "I *lost* the admiral."

"I bet if you asked Pierre, he'd do it," suggested Ophelia.

Matilda adjusted the crocheted tablecloth. "You don't think it would seem *insensitive* to the Jones' family?"

"Not if we wait a suitable amount of time for mourning."

"Do you really think Pierre would do it? I've asked for his help several times before but he declined."

Ophelia tapped the side of her nose. "I'll have a word."

This suggestion appeared to go a long way to improving Matilda's dour mood. "It will take him some time to learn his lines, of course. In a week or two, we'll have another rehearsal with Pierre and see if I think he's ready."

The decisive reversal of her state of mind made it clear that Matilda had given no thought to the fact that the poison had not hit the correct mark. *Best to let sleeping dogs lie.*

The newer school was built three hundred years after the village, but the architects had tried to maintain the Elizabethan style. The structure consisted of a rather long building with small classrooms at either end of an assembly hall. School ended at half past three and the bell was ringing as they approached. Within seconds, children of all ages were rushing past them as they entered the corridor which led to the headmistress's office.

Judith sat, eyes closed, as if meditating.

Ophelia cleared her throat.

Judith recoiled.

She let out a sigh of relief on seeing the twins in front of her desk. "To what do I owe this honor?"

Imogen pulled up a chair. "We need to talk to you about a delicate matter."

Judith leaned forward, elbows on the desk. "You're here to warn me that I may have been the real object of the killer's poison."

Judith Rutherford had become a teacher at a young age, in Somerset. Taking a leave of absence, she had served as a nurse during the war, an experience that prepared her well for the many demands placed on a village school headmistress.

And she was nobody's fool.

"Once I got home, the night of the dress rehearsal, I couldn't sleep. I had a vivid image of Mildred holding that bottle she found in the bin, and it hit me. The poison was in the glass. The prop on the table during the dinner scene with the ladies. I remembered how it sloshed on Alice's dress which was unexpected because they were supposed to be empty for the rehearsal." She looked up. "The poison was supposed to kill one of us."

"I'm afraid you're right." Ophelia pushed her lips out in a gesture of pity. "Is there anyone you suspect of targeting you?"

Ophelia watched as Judith's normally composed demeanor cracked ever so slightly. The headmistress's hand went to her throat, and her eyes took on that distant look of those who were remembering experiences from the war. When she finally spoke, her voice was unsteady.

"I've given it a lot of thought. There was one soldier who died under my care. Obviously, it happened all the time, it was war, and some of the wounds were horrific. But this particular soldier was a gentleman, and he had a fiancée, a fiancée who happened to be carrying his child. She could not accept that he died, as it left her open to a great deal of scorn. She was so angry and I was a convenient scapegoat. She wrote me some quite terrible letters. I burned them. I understood it was part of her grief, but I'd be lying if I said they had no effect." The headmistress leaned back, her mind still in the past. "I often wonder what happened to her. The child would be eleven years old by now."

"But you haven't heard from her since the end of the war?"

"No. I half think she wanted me to react, to throw a fit and write some spiteful denial back. It might have given her comfort in a strange way. But I chose to stay above the fray."

"I suppose if she were rejected by her family and found herself on the street, so to speak, she might blame you? And this would be an age that an upper-class son might be sent away to an expensive boarding school."

"True. I had the very same thought myself. But in her saner moments, the woman had to know there was nothing a mere nurse could have done to save him. We cared for the men but the doctors operated on them. If she wanted to blame anyone, it should have been a doctor. Both the soldier's legs were shot off and he'd lost so much blood by the time we got him. The truth was, he was already dying when he arrived at the hospital tent at the front. It was a miracle he made it back to the hospital in England at all."

"And you can think of no one else? What about your time in Russia?" On another of their cases they had learned that Judith had been part of a teacher exchange to Russia, right before the revolution.

She shook her head. "I was so young. So naïve. There was a young man at the school who walked me home to my lodgings every day. But we were only friends. Nothing came of it. I had already been home for six months when the revolution began. He sent me a gift some time after I left, but since then, we've lost touch."

"Just friends?" Ophelia pressed gently.

Judith's eyes grew distant again. "Well... perhaps he hoped for more. Mikhail was his name. He taught mathematics. He had such dreams for the new Russia he believed was coming." She twisted a watch at her wrist. "The last message I received from him spoke of great changes ahead. Then the revolution came, and all communication came to an end. Sometimes I wonder if he even survived those early days."

"Is it possible he could have found you after all these years?

"I suppose it's possible. But we were *friends*." She lifted her hand in supplication. "Mikhail would have no reason to kill me. No, I think the soldier's fiancée is more likely. Grief *can* curdle into something dangerous over the years but, like I said, if that young woman wanted to blame someone, it would have been the doctors or the Germans. She would have realized that with time."

"All the same, you should mind your back."

"I thought the same thing. And there's one strange thing that's happened. Now, I can't be absolutely sure, and I wouldn't have given it a second thought but for the murder, but a couple of days before the death, I had the impression a stranger had been in my house and moved some things. Upon reflection, it's made me a little nervous, so I've invited my sister Agnes to come and stay." Judith rose, gathering her things. "She arrives on tomorrow afternoon's train."

"Good," Ophelia bobbed her head. "And in the meantime, perhaps you should stay at the vicarage? Or with us, though you'd have to sleep on the sofa."

"That's very kind, but I'll manage. I survived a field hospital during the war—I'm hardly a defenseless child anymore." She pulled a small revolver from her handbag. "A souvenir from my nursing days. I keep it in my desk at home but given the circumstances, thought I'd carry it with me."

She showed the twins to the door. "Thank you for coming to warn me. Did the others realize the same thing?"

Ophelia stepped across the threshold and turned back. "No. They were rather unnerved when we told them."

"I'll call Kitty. She's a newcomer and lives alone. She may not have many friends in the village yet. I'll invite her to stay with me and my sister until this is all over." Judith closed the door to her office and locked it with a key.

"She's made arrangements to stay with another teacher in Willowbrook," said Imogen, "but she might like your offer better."

As the twins walked home in the gathering dusk, Ophelia gave voice to her thoughts.

"Four women, four possible motives, and somewhere lurking in the village, a killer who's already tried once ..."

"And is sure to try again," Imogen finished grimly.

CHAPTER 17

Ghost Town

Ophelia was on edge.

It had been four days since the attempt on one of the women's lives. Had the murderer left in shame and horror that they had killed the wrong person never to return, or were they so cruel and calculating that they were willing to wait until the community had let down their guard?

The frightening truth that Farmer Jones had not been the target of the murderer's poison had finally weaved itself into the tapestry of the village gossip vine. People who had known each other for years, eyed one another askance as they passed on the pavement.

Believing the danger level to be high, the chief constable of Parkford had loaned the village three plain clothes policemen and two extra constables. But how long would the extra police presence last? Inspector Southam had made a request for witnesses who had noticed any strangers in the village in the days running up to the murder. Unfortunately, this only gave him a hundred false sightings from skittish folks imagining things.

Sales in the stores plummeted as people stayed home in fear.

But Imogen needed jam. Toast without jam was not to be

tolerated. She took Tiger along and tied him to a lamppost outside *Tumblethhorn's.*

"Mrs. Pettigrew!" cried Reggie, today wearing a top hat and tails. "You've saved me from death by boredom. I'm begging you to come and talk to me before I go mad." He clasped soft hands under his chin. "Please!"

She was more than happy to oblige. Reggie was a lovely chap about the same age as her son Fergus, but whereas her son was terribly unassuming, Reggie's personality hit every color of the spectrum; you never quite knew what he was going to do or say.

"What special do you have this week, Reggie?"

He pinched the edges of a bowtie made of scarlet, polka dot satin. "A chappie sold me a box lot for an absolute steal. I thought I'd advertise them by donning my dinner jacket. What do you think?"

It would be impolitic to tell him what she really thought. "Well, it's very bright. Nice on a gloomy day like this."

Reggie clapped his hands. "That's almost exactly what mother said." He rearranged a display of throat lozenges that sat by the cash register, and his features into a caricature of a gossip. "I assume you and your sister are on the case?"

She leaned an elbow on the counter. "Since we were there when it happened, we feel it our duty to help the police. Did they ask you in for a second interview?"

"Oh, yes. The day after the murder. I was an absolute wreck. I've never seen anyone die right in front of me." Though Imogen knew that he had discovered a dead body in the woods some years ago. "I could barely remember anything. I think it was the shock. I made an awful witness. Totally useless."

"What did you say?"

"I told the inspector that I ran the table off stage with the other chaps and watched from the wings as the blokes on the other side brought on the promenade railings. I described Nicholas stumbling around and clutching his throat—or was it his chest? Look at me!" He grabbed both sides of the hat. "I still don't remember."

She checked that Tiger was behaving. "Do you recall which men helped with the table?"

Reggie crossed his arms, lifting a finger to his chin. "Let me see ... Des Ale and Molly's boys, Mark and David. We were standing in a group when Farmer Jones went down."

She considered the three names. Des had been through a lot the last few years and was a thoroughly decent person. According to their parents, the two young men from Manchester were settling in but missing home.

"Can you remember anything about the glass?"

"Funny you should say that." Reggie removed the hat. Tufts of hair stood up on end. "During my second interview it occurred to me that some of the liquid splashed over the sides and got on my trousers as we carried the table off. At the time, I thought I'd suggest a dedicated person to remove the full glasses for the actual performance. Then Nicolas went down and I forgot all about it." He leaned over the counter and stared into Imogen's eyes. "Do you realize that if I'd wiped that wet patch with my hand, then put it to my mouth, I could have died too." The terror had caused his voice to rise.

"What's that?" croaked his fragile mother from the sitting room in the back of the shop.

His face and shoulders dropped into a guilty shrug. "Nothing, Mother!"

It was true. Reggie could have died or at the very least, been violently ill. Both he *and* Alice. *Alice.* Imogen decided that since she was out, she would pay a visit to her friend, the baker, after she had finished at the grocer's.

And there was one point in all this that still bothered her. How could there be no witnesses? "You didn't see anyone who shouldn't have been back there, in the wings, did you?"

Reggie's anxious eyes studied the ceiling. "It was rather chaotic, as you'd expect, but I don't remember being surprised and anyway, the killer would have fled right after putting the stuff in the glass, wouldn't they?"

"Yes, Reggie. They'd have been long gone after sneaking into the lavatories to throw the bottle in the bin."

She flashed back to Mildred holding the bottle aloft by the ladies' toilet door. *Did that mean the murderer was a woman?*

The Golden Crust Bakery was empty too. Usually, the line for the Puddingfield's baked goods was out the door. Imogen rang the bell on the counter.

"Imogen." Archie hurried into the shop front while tying on his white apron. "It's been so quiet, I was having a cuppa in the back room."

"No need to apologize. The whole village is like a ghost town. Tiger is wondering where everyone is. He misses the attention."

"Everyone is spooked and with good reason. No one goes out unless they absolutely have to. I had to throw out a boatload of bread yesterday. I hope people start coming out soon or we'll have a very slim month."

It would be the same for all the shopkeepers. Their livelihoods depended on people spending money.

"I'll take a cobb loaf, please. Is Alice home?"

Archie grabbed a loaf, wrapped it in butcher paper and called for his wife. She entered the shop front with a look of anticipation on her pretty face and a dash of flour on the end of her nose.

"Imogen! How lovely to see you."

"I needed some jam and when you have jam, you need fresh bread."

"Thank heavens! We only had two customers yesterday and you're the first today."

Tiger barked at a shred of newspaper that rolled by in the wind.

"It's understandable," said Imogen. "Especially now everyone knows Farmer Jones' death was an accident."

Alice bit her lip. "I even got to wondering if it was supposed to be *me* that died." She brushed the hair from her face with an arm. "Daft really. Who'd want to kill me?"

Archie's face hardened. "What? You never told me."

"I didn't want you to worry, dear."

"Well, I'm officially worried."

Imogen decided not to mention that if Alice had touched the wet spot on her dress after the spill, it could well have been her. But she had come here to move the investigation forward.

"Ophelia and I believe the cyanide was intended for one of the ladies at the table in the dinner scene."

Alice froze. "Celina, Kitty, Molly or Judith? I thought as much, but you shut down that theory the day of the murder."

Ophelia glanced at Tiger who was trying to catch dead leaves in his mouth. "I'm sorry but people were already nervy and I didn't want to cause a wave of hysteria. As you realized that night, the glasses were used in the leading ladies' dinner scene."

"I thought I must have been wrong, and since then, I've been too busy worrying it was me they were after." She chuckled then got serious. "Have you told them?"

Imogen reached for the loaf and put it in her basket. "Yes. If the murderer botched the attempt, they could try again."

Alice shivered as Imogen handed her the change. "Then I don't know how they sleep, especially since three of them are single!"

"Judith has invited Kitty to stay at her cottage with she and her sister, who arrived today. Celina is staying with her mother till this all blows over."

One of the mother's from the crescent hurried past with her children. Tiger strained at the lead holding him.

"It was never like this before the war, was it Archie?"

He huffed. "We didn't even lock our doors. We do now."

"Lucky for you to have Tiger." Alice looked out the glass door at the German shepherd who finally lay on the ground, sulking.

"We are, and he's such a good boy." Imogen shifted the wicker basket to her other arm. "Did the police talk to you again?"

"No." Alice stiffened. "Should I expect another call?"

"Only if they were dissatisfied with the first interview or some new evidence comes to light." She looked at the display of buns and her mouth began to water. "Oh, go on then. I'll take two currant buns for our tea."

Archie took tongs and placed the buns in a paper bag.

"Do you remember who was on your side of the stage when the table went out?" she asked Alice.

"Me. All the leading ladies, the two mischief makers, Collin and Tommy, and Ed Sugden. He and the boys took the table out. Then there was Mildred and Patricia. They took the other glasses out. Pru was standing in the wings to give direction and prompt anyone who forgot their lines."

"Sounds crowded."

"It was."

Which means anybody could easily have sneaked the toxic substance into the glass without anyone noticing. But how did they manage to get the poison bottle into the lavatory bin with no witnesses? In the chaos that followed the death, she supposed they could have run to the toilets and back in a moment and no one would have been any the wiser.

While Archie wrapped the buns, Imogen asked about that night.

Alice wiped floury hands on her apron, her brow furrowing. "As I said, I've been over and over it and I did realize that someone slipped down the back stairs as we were getting the props on stage."

Ophelia felt hopeful. "Was it a woman or a man?"

"Honestly, it could have been either, I only really saw the door swing closed out of the corner of my eye." Her eyes widened. "And there was something else. As I looked out from the wings, I noticed the men's lavatory door was ajar, which was odd because Pru had locked both doors earlier in the evening because the boys kept going in and making a mess, and Rex had complained. If anyone needed to go, they had to ask Pru for the key."

Imogen's pulse quickened. "Do you remember what time that was?"

"It must have been just before the dinner scene. I remember because I was helping Molly fix her wig during the previous scene change, and she kept fussing about being late for her cue."

"*Before* the dinner scene?" Imogen leaned forward. "And

you're certain about the lavatory door? Did you mention it to the police?"

"I didn't remember it then. It was just another detail in a crazy evening." Alice twisted her apron between her fingers.

Archie, who had been listening intently, suddenly spoke up. "That reminds *me* of something I didn't think much of at the time. I saw a person walking away from the back of the hall as I was taking the rubbish out. It was as the rehearsal started. I just caught a glimpse. They weren't in a hurry or anything."

The sound of barking outside made them all jump. Through the shop window, they could see the dog standing alert, the hair on his back raised, his attention fixed on something out of their sight.

Imogen rushed to the door, but whoever had caught the hound's attention had disappeared. The dog settled back down, though his ears remained pricked.

Could the person Archie had noticed that night be a stranger who had slipped in and out of the hall unnoticed during the bedlam of scene changes? *Jack Scroggins? Bob Sugden?* No, it could not be a stranger. It was someone who knew exactly where the props would be.

The bell on the door tinkled.

Mildred.

Imogen stiffened.

"Oh, if it isn't half of the pair of self-proclaimed detectives."

"Mildred," said Archie, making an effort to diffuse the situation. "What can I get for you?"

She reached into her bag and pulled out a piece of paper. "I was hoping you would put this up in your window."

Imogen managed to lay eyes on the bulletin as Mildred handed it to Archie.

A fundraiser for the Jones' family.

Just when Imogen wanted to dismiss Mildred as nothing more than a nasty gossip and a busybody, she did something kind that showed her better nature. Despite her sharp tongue and talent for stirring up trouble, Mildred *could* show real compassion, such as this effort to rally the village to show an outpouring of support for the victim's family. It was a pointed reminder that people rarely fit into neat categories of good and bad.

Mildred spun to face Imogen. "Do you know anything we don't already?"

"A little, but I'm not at liberty to share it at the present time."

Mildred huffed. "And I think it very poor judgement on the part of the police not to tell us *immediately* that Farmer Jones was not the intended target. How can we protect ourselves if we're kept in the dark?"

"You'll have to take that up with the inspector." Imogen headed for the door. "By the way, did you need a key to get into the ladies' that night?"

"No, it was open. Why?" Mildred's sharp features stood to attention as did the stuffed bird on her hat.

"No reason. I don't suppose you saw anyone in the lavatory earlier in the evening, did you?"

Irritation bristled across Mildred's face. "No. Are you accusing me of planting the bottle?"

Imogen reached for the door handle. "Not at all. I was just wondering if it was all in order?"

"Are you asking me about finding the poison?"

"I suppose I am. How did you come across it, exactly? Was it just lying at the top of the rubbish bin?"

"If you must know, I dropped the brooch from my costume as I bent over to check my face in the mirror, and it went into the bin. Fell all the way to the bottom. I had to rummage around inside to find the brooch and that's when I came upon the bottle. It was wrapped in newspaper and tucked into the bottom of the container. If I'd not accidentally dropped the jewelry, we may never have found the poison."

Like a cat who has found the cream, Mildred's face reflected an arrogant expression, as though she felt she deserved a medal for blowing the case open. Imogen held her tongue, but sorely wanted to point out that the police would have turned the place upside down after they left and found the bottle of cyanide in the course of their investigations.

"And you're sure there was no one else in the toilets?"

"No. Rex Stout had just cleaned it and warned us to keep the place tidy. What's all this interest in the ladies' toilets, anyway?"

"Nothing," said Imogen opening the door. "You're doing a really nice thing raising money for the Joneses."

Mildred preened. "This is exactly the kind of thing the WI should be doing. I'm sure I can count on your support."

Imogen was about to respond when Tiger's bark split the air again. Through the bakery window, she saw the lead pulled tight against the lamppost, the dog focused on something. Stepping out the door, Prudence practically ran into her.

"What on earth's wrong?" Imogen asked as she unhooked Tiger's lead.

Panting, Pru put a hand to her chest. "It's Judith. I've j-just come from the school and am on my way to the p-police station. Oh, Imogen! She's been poisoned."

CHAPTER 18

A Narrow Escape

Imogen dropped the basket.

Dread settled in her bones. Hadn't she and Ophelia warned all the interested parties? Hadn't the police upped their presence? Still, the killer had succeeded.

How could this have happened? Fear coiled in her stomach.

"Go!" Imogen managed, her voice barely above a whisper, as the hurried steps of the vicar's wife faded. Tiger pressed against her leg with an anxious whine. Imogen looked down at him, but her mind's eye saw only Judith's body sprawled across the polished office floor.

The dog jerked his lead, the sudden movement snapping her back to the present. Leaning into the bakery, she informed her worried friends of the dire events.

"No!" cried Alice.

Archie placed a comforting arm around his wife, but his expression was anything but calm.

"Call Ophelia. Tell her to meet me at the school."

"Will do." Archie's face was as pale as the flour of his trade.

Imogen fumbled with the knot on the lead but finally got it undone, then walked as fast as her legs would carry her. Tiger raised his head, eyes filled with confusion at their speed.

Why did she feel so guilty? What more could they have done? She chided herself; no one was responsible for this calamity but the murderer.

Panting as she approached, the school stood serene in the afternoon light, its peaceful facade betraying nothing of the drama unfolding within. The empty playground lay silent as a tomb.

Pushing through the school doors, Imogen set her course for the office where she and Ophelia had met with the headmistress just two days before. Tiger's nose quivered with excitement as he pulled her along, drawn to the children's scents lingering in the corridor. Imogen scolded him, guiding the dog down the hall, past classrooms where the innocent bustle of daily school life stood in stark contrast to the gravity of what had occurred just yards away.

In the back office, Mrs. Ledger, the school secretary, knelt by the body of Judith Rutherford, her homely face strained with grief.

A hair-raising, yet glorious, retching broke the silence, and the headmistress lurched forward, emptying her stomach across the secretary's neat navy skirt.

"I gave her ipecac syrup," sobbed Mrs. Ledger, ignoring the vomit.

The headmistress slammed back against the ground. The secretary ripped off her cardigan, bunching it into a makeshift pillow, and placing it under Judith's head.

Tiger sniffed the air as the acid tang of the vomit made its way across the room. Imogen ran to the prostrate headmistress and felt her wrist.

"It's thready but it's there," she cried with relief. "Well done, Mrs. Ledger!"

The exhausted secretary slumped against the side of the desk.

"Now let's get you cleaned up. I'll stay with Judith."

Tiger curled up beside the prostrate patient as Imogen kept checking the headmistress's pulse and watching for the slight rise and fall of her chest. Every minute of waiting for help to arrive seemed like an eternity.

At length, Tiger pricked up his ears as the sound of heavy boots on parquet floor preceded the explosion of four policemen into the room. Two of them carried a primitive stretcher. Constable Hargrove barked orders and the three policemen from Parkford lifted the ailing headmistress onto the stretcher then hurried out to a waiting police van.

"I thought we'd come for a corpse," the constable gasped, pulling at the chin strap of his helmet. "But as soon as I saw you and Tiger and caught that stink in the air, I knew the mission had changed. Good job we brought the van."

"Prescient, Constable," replied Imogen feeling emotionally wiped out. "All the credit goes to Mrs. Ledger. It was she who administered the ipecac syrup. Her quick thinking likely saved Miss Rutherford's life."

The constable examined the half empty cup on the desk and the chair sitting askew. "Looks like the poison was in her tea. I'll need to ask Mrs. Ledger about that."

"She's just tidying herself up. I'm sure she'll return momentarily."

Released from his self-directed duty of guarding the sick patient, Tiger circled the room restlessly, his nose working overtime, before settling into an oddly intense inspection of the skirting board next to the headmistress's desk. Imogen squatted down to see a faint smudge. Upon closer inspection she decided it was a heavier smear of some kind of oil or grease that had been hastily wiped. She leaned in and caught a hint of cleaning solution. It was strangely familiar.

At that moment, Ophelia appeared at the door, cheeks flushed from her brisk trek across the common. Imogen stood and felt the ridiculous urge to fling herself into her sister's arms and cry like a baby.

"She's alive." It was a statement rather than a question.

"Yes," replied Imogen, her words weak from worry.

Ophelia strode across the room, past Imogen and Tiger, making straight for the cup. She sniffed. "Bitter almonds."

"I'll be taking that to send to the lab in Parkford," said the constable, fingering the truncheon hanging from his belt.

Noticing a diary on the desk, Ophelia searched the headmistress's appointments for the day. She'd had a meeting with some parents in the morning, but nothing was scheduled for the afternoon.

Mrs. Ledger reappeared, her hair awry and skirt wet.

Ophelia seized the opportunity. "I know you've had a difficult afternoon, but do you mind if I ask you some questions while everything is fresh in your mind?"

The secretary's hand went to her hair. "Of course. Anything to help."

"According to her calendar, Miss Rutherford had no appointments this afternoon. Did anyone come in without one?"

"No. We were busy with a plumbing problem in the boy's bathroom. Miss Rutherford's a dab hand at most stuff, but she couldn't get the leak to stop, so we called Mr. Stout to pop over and help. He had it sorted out in a jiffy. Other than that, it was a quiet afternoon."

"And you made the tea?"

"No. That *is* a mystery. Miss Rutherford doesn't take tea in the afternoon unless she's seeing parents. I make her tea at eleven, then she waits until the children have gone home and makes it herself." She glanced at the clock. "Good heavens! I'm late with the bell. Please excuse me."

She grabbed the bell sitting on a credenza and rushed into the hall. Within seconds, the peal of the bell echoed through the halls and mere seconds after that, the classrooms coughed up their students. Children stampeded through the corridors, streaming toward home or hovering mothers. In a surprisingly short time, the halls returned to their silent state.

While the secretary was gone, Ophelia studied the office more thoroughly. Judith's desk told its own story - scattered progress reports, a draft of a letter to parents about the upcoming spring festival, a small photograph of her nursing unit from the war in a silver frame. Everything spoke of a life interrupted mid-task.

The frazzled Mrs. Ledger returned, placing the hefty bell back in its place. "Now, where were we?" She made another halfhearted effort to smooth her hair in a futile attempt to tame the wild strands.

Ophelia pointed to the cup. "You were saying you didn't make tea this afternoon and yet there's a cup of it on Miss Rutherford's desk."

"Oh, yes." She dragged both hands down her worn features. "She must have worked up a thirst with the plumbing and made it for herself."

"Is there any chance she could have left the room while the cup was sitting here?"

Mrs. Ledger made a noise that under better circumstances would have been a real chuckle. "That woman rarely sits for more than two minutes at a time. She's always being called to sort out some problem or another. There's every chance she would have left the room." She sniffed and took a handkerchief out of her sleeve. Dabbing at her eyes she said, "I've been at this school for twelve years, you know. Started as a young widow with a child to support." She glanced out the window as she wandered down memory lane. "Miss Trumble—she was headmistress then—took me on, despite my lack of experience. Said she knew what it was to make your own way in the world."

She smoothed her ruined skirt with trembling hands. "When Miss Trumble died, we all worried about what sort of person would replace her. The children were nervous – especially little Billy Barnes who has trouble with his reading. But Miss Rutherford ..." Her voice caught. "First day here, she called Billy into her office and sat with him for an hour after school, just talking about the pictures in his book. Now he's reading better than half his class."

Moving into the adjoining office to her own desk, she picked up a small wooden box. "She gave me this at Christmas. Said she'd noticed my old pencil box was falling apart." Lifting the lid revealed neat compartments for pens and pencils. "That's the sort of person she is, always noticing what others need.

When Mary Clark's mother was ill, do you know she walked the girl home from school every day for a week. And when one of the other mothers couldn't afford new shoes for her twins, a package mysteriously showed up on her doorstep. I know because the woman came here in tears to say thank you because one of the neighbors had seen Miss Rutherford drop them off." A tear splashed onto the wooden box. "And now someone's tried to... to..." She couldn't finish the sentence.

"There, there," said Imogen placing an arm around the distraught woman. "You saved her life."

After a couple of minutes, the constable cleared his throat, notebook at the ready. "Did you see any strangers hanging around the school today?"

Biting her lips, Mrs. Ledger shook her head.

He stepped past her to inspect the wastepaper bin. This time there was no incriminating evidence. "Right. If you wouldn't mind, I'd like to take your official statement."

They exited the back office, and the twin sisters and Tiger congregated in the passageway. Ophelia wrapped Imogen in a sisterly embrace.

"Not the way I wanted to find out who the intended victim was."

"No, indeed." Imogen's eyes were prickling with tears. "I feel as though we messed up."

Ophelia pulled back. "Nonsense! The killer deserves all the blame. Don't you waste one minute on self-recrimination. This is *not* our fault. We warned all the possible targets, which frankly, was more than the police have done."

"That's true and they had *all* taken precautions. No one could have foreseen the attack being made at the school under the nose of all the children."

Making their way slowly back through the corridor, Ophelia and Imogen passed empty classrooms that seemed frozen in time. Cheerful artwork adorned the walls – spring flowers painted in bright watercolors, carefully copied alphabet letters. Through open doors, they saw half-finished lessons still chalked on blackboards while teachers sat at their desks marking papers, as yet, unaware of the attack on their headmistress.

Ophelia slipped her arm through Imogen's. "At least now we can direct our attention in the proper direction. We need to find out what became of that young Russian teacher. If he was pro-revolution, he may have been more indoctrinated than Judith realized. Who knows what he may have done after she left the country?"

"And the soldier's fiancée," Imogen added, absently stroking Tiger's ears. "Perhaps it's time to press harder about those letters Judith burned. There might have been clues in them about the woman's whereabouts."

Ophelia pushed open the school door with renewed determination. "I have some contacts in the home office who might have information about the soldier's vital records. Those might lead us to the desperate fiancée. And while I'm at it, I can ask if they have any files on the Russian, any record of him crossing the channel into the country or anything of that sort."

"While you work on that, I can ask Judith for the name of the Russian school she worked at, when she's recovered a bit, of course. Then I can send a telegram. It was only twelve years ago. There's bound to be people around who remember them. If we're lucky, this man will still be teaching there, and we can strike him from our list of suspects."

Ophelia stepped over a discarded skipping rope. "Here's the thing that really worries me. The murderer will be positively desperate after two failed attempts."

"At least Judith's safe in hospital," Imogen said as they turned toward home.

"Let's hope so, ducky. Let's hope so."

CHAPTER 19

The Past and Present Collide

Due to a bargain Ophelia had struck during another case, she had played at the private birthday party of the mother of Sir William Blankley, to wild acclaim. She had to admit, although she enjoyed retirement, she missed the thrill of performing. The solo concert, in front of a small crowd of elites, had scratched her itch satisfactorily. Furthermore, it had provided an excellent opportunity to rub shoulders with former friends from another life who might prove to be valuable assets in the future.

"Billy! It's me, Ophelia."

"Ophelia! Good to hear from you. Mother is still talking about your amazing performance. Your ability to make the violin sing is equal to none."

"I appreciate the accolade. Look, I'll get right to the point. I know you're an important and busy man so I'm hoping you can hook me up with someone far lower down the ladder who might be able to help me find information on a Russian revolutionary who may have come into the country."

"Great Scott, woman! What have you got yourself mixed up with now?" He ended his question with a loud guffaw.

"We're having a little trouble in my neck of the woods, and it may involve a Russian again. I'm sure it will be in all the papers soon enough."

"Can't let it go, huh? Retirement too tame for you?"

"You know how it is," she admitted. "Can you give me a name and an endorsement?"

"Of course." He recited a name and number with a promise to give the man a warning to expect her. "Is that all?"

"Actually ..."

"Out with it!"

"I need some information on a soldier who died in the war. How would I find his vital records?"

He gave her another name and number.

"Thank you, Billy. I owe you one!"

"Yes, you do."

She hung up the phone with a smile.

"Did you get the information we need?" asked Imogen over lunch.

"Are you up for another trip to London?" Ophelia winked.

"In February? I'd better pack heavy."

"And I'll call Peter to take care of the dog. We'll need to be gone overnight as the person we need to talk to about the Russian is in Whitehall, and the soldier who died, was from Hampstead Heath. I think that conversation is better done face to face."

"Can you ask your neighbor to get a fire going? I was freezing the last time we stayed at your apartment."

"Good idea. I'll give her a call.

They managed to catch the two o'clock fast train to London and arrived in the capital around half-past three.

Ophelia hailed a taxi. "I made an appointment with Mr. Graham at Whitehall for four o'clock. We'll seek out the soldier's family tomorrow morning."

Whitehall appeared rather gray as the damp overcast weather offered it no light. Imogen was grateful the government building felt warm compared with the street outside. A fussy looking woman checked them off on her list and sent them to a door down a long, dark corridor.

"Come in!" ordered a reedy voice.

The man who received them was impossibly tall and thin and wore pince-nez on the very end of a long nose. He stood, holding out his hand, a wry smile on his face at the identical women before him.

"Any friend of Billy Blankley is a friend of mine," he said, revealing large, stained teeth. "Please sit." He threaded his fingers on the desk. "Which one of you is Miss Harrington?"

"Guilty," said Ophelia, one lip hitching into a grin.

"Now, let me see if I understand the problem. A murderer has made two attempts to kill your friend but been unsuccessful. This pal of yours taught in Russia a little before the revolution, and became involved with a Russian teacher named Mikhail Martov, who at that time had Bolshevik leanings. That about the long and short of it?"

Impressive!

"You've hit the nail clean on the head, sir."

Reaching long fingers into a bottom drawer, he pulled out a thick file. Imogen easily saw that the file was named after the man in question.

"Though this person is not known to me personally, there is an agency you may be familiar with, that is more than aware of him." He opened the file and took out a sheet of typed paper.

"I assume you don't have long to peruse the file, and I admit, it did peak my interest, so I took notes and had my secretary type them up. It goes without saying that most of this is classified but since he is a suspect in a murder investigation, I have permission to share certain facts with you."

Ophelia held the paper up so that Imogen could read it too.

"I'll give you the short version, then I'll leave to go and chase down some pesky paperwork on another matter." He peered over the pince-nez. "It will not be possible to let that paper leave this office, but what you do with it in my absence is up to you." He made a pyramid with his bony hands. "This Martov became an important member of Lenin's government, having performed certain errands for him at the start of the revolution. He enjoyed an elevated status for several years but Lenin is a fickle master. He lost Lenin's favor and his name was placed on a blacklist. Escape was imperative. We believe he accomplished this through cutting across Croatia then up through Italy. Not finding the atmosphere friendly, he continued up through France and settled in Brittany."

He plucked the pipe that rested in a holder and clamped it between his teeth.

"Unfortunately for Martov, his enemies located his whereabouts, and he was forced to flee again, this time to the British Isles under the assumed name of Trevor Bates. It's easy to get lost in London, which he achieved admirably for many years, until he was recognized by a British spy. You can imagine how the presence of a known member of Lenin's government in London, might rock the boat. He was forced to go into hiding again. MI5 surveilled his haunts knowing he would need to earn his bread, but thus far, he has avoided all efforts to locate him."

Mr. Graham struck a match and puffed into the pipe as he lit the tobacco.

"You should be aware there are plenty of people interested to know that he may have come up for breath in Meadowshire."

The twins stared at each other as Mr. Graham left the room with his pipe.

"Another Russian spy in Meadowshire!" gasped Imogen.

"It would seem it's a good place to hide."

They scanned the paper and Ophelia read portions that Imogen wrote down. There were files from Italy, France and England on the man. His past was dark, full of people around him disappearing permanently. The methods of execution, described by those who had informants inside Russia, were sickening and Imogen felt her stomach roll.

"What a thoroughly repellent man. It's a good thing Judith didn't continue her relationship with him."

Ophelia stopped. "I thought you'd have learned better by now, ducky. People lie."

Imogen let the pencil drop. "You think Judith is still in contact with him and he tried to kill her in case she outed him?"

"I like it better than any of our other theories, don't you?"

"I certainly prefer it to one of our friends being the murderer. I've had quite enough of that."

Ophelia tapped the paper. "And cyanide poisoning is one of the methods listed here. Martov would be an expert in keeping a low profile. Yes, this feels like we might be on to something."

By the time Mr. Graham returned, they had jotted down all the salient points. He slipped the synopsis back into the file and glanced at his watch.

His smile was as slim as his face. "It was very nice to meet you, but my five o'clock has just arrived."

"Of course, We'll get out of your hair. I can't thank you enough." They shook hands again and he led them to the door.

Outside, sitting on a chair in the hall, was a roguish fellow with amber eyes and a dimple in his chin. Ophelia almost squeaked. Instead, she flared her eyes and almost imperceptibly shook her head.

The individual merely nodded at the twins and entered Mr. Graham's room.

"Did you know him?" asked Imogen.

"Why would you think that?" responded Ophelia, eyes straight ahead.

"I thought I saw a flash of recognition in his face when he saw you."

Imogen was extraordinarily perceptive sometimes.

"No. Perhaps we look like someone else he knows. Do you fancy a cream tea?"

Warmth from the fire Ophelia's neighbor had built spilled into the hallway as she opened her apartment door. Inside, souvenirs from her many travels adorned the walls and shelves, while shabby, colorful furniture invited relaxation.

Imogen removed her coat and fell into an armchair by the fire.

"I don't have any food," remarked Ophelia. "I'll just pop out before the shops close and get some milk and bread. Do you want to come?"

"Do you mind if I don't?" The last thing Imogen wanted to do was go back out into the cold.

"Of course not. There are more blankets in a basket in my bedroom if you get chilly. I'll be back in a jiffy."

Imogen struggled out of the chair in search of the blankets before she got too settled. As she bent over, the solitaire pearl necklace she wore, fell to the wooden floor and the highly valuable gray pearl rolled under the bed.

"*Hot crumpets!*" she complained, dropping to all fours. Though the necklace was not as precious to her as the locket she always wore, the pearl had been a gift from her late husband and she had no intention of letting it fall through any cracks in the floorboards. Letting her fingers walk through trails of cobwebs and dust, they dropped into a light indentation in the floor. Curious, she went back to the living room to get the small flashlight she always carried in her handbag.

This time, she rolled onto her side, flashing the beam under the bed. The rays of light picked up the sheen on the pearl and she hyper-extended her arm, curling her hand to retrieve the lost trinket. However, instead of rolling toward her, the jewel fell into the indentation she had felt before. Stretching her index finger to get a better grip, she touched something else. Was it a latch? Spinning the pearl toward her, she slid it back on the chain, re-clasping the necklace around her neck. Then she laid on the floor again, clawing for the latch and pulled. The floorboard moved.

This is prying. Stop! Go back to the living room.

But the discovery felt like the last piece of a puzzle that had been forming, almost unintentionally, since she and her sister had started living together. The way Ophelia seemed to know Pierre's history, how she could pick locks so deftly, the 'friends' she had in high places who helped them when no one else could. And finally, today, the manner in which that gentleman outside

Mr. Graham's office had recognized her, then pretended not to.

Ophelia was keeping something from her. Imogen was her twin. She *deserved* to know.

Unable to get any traction, she nudged the bed a foot, revealing the loose board. Ophelia would be back soon. It was now or never.

Jimmying the floorboard with a nail file from her purse, she managed to dislodge the plank and pull it out, revealing a metal box beneath. She flashed back to their first case where the suspect had hidden important documents under the floorboards. Perhaps that was all that was here, and she was barking up the wrong tree. But she *had* to know. She withdrew the box and opened the lid.

On the top was an old photograph of a much younger Pierre standing next to a youthful Ophelia. The backdrop was the Colosseum in Rome. She picked it up and flipped it over. A date was written on the back.

The hair on her neck rose as she found a small leather wallet under the snapshot, containing a credential of some kind on cream-colored, heavy card. On the upper portion was a formal portrait photograph of Ophelia before her hair turned gray. Rather than a name, a number identified the photograph, below which was a government seal bearing the royal coat of arms.

Imogen's world tilted on its axis.

In a daze, she flicked through the other items. On top lay newspaper clippings about diplomatic incidents across the continent. Beneath them, wrapped in silk, lay a medal Imogen had never seen before – not for musical achievement, but for service to the Crown.

A conclusion began to draw itself in her mind, but she swatted it away. It was impossible, wasn't it?

Lifting the silk, she gasped as a simple, gold wedding ring winked at her in the light.

"I'm back!" cried Ophelia, crashing through the apartment door, the fall of her footsteps headed for the tiny kitchen. "Where are you?"

Imogen could not speak.

She sat frozen, the damning evidence spread before her. The cheerful rustle of paper bags and the ordinary domestic sounds of Ophelia arriving home seemed to belong to another world entirely – a world in which her sister was simply a retired violinist, not ... not whatever *this* meant she was.

"I managed to get the last loaf," Ophelia called from the other side of the bedroom door. "And Mrs. Pembroke asked after you..."

Her voice trailed off as she opened the door to the bedroom. The scarlet scarf she had been holding pooled red as blood at her feet.

For a long moment, neither of them spoke.

Imogen looked at Ophelia and saw a stranger.

She still clutched the small leather folder, her knuckles aching with tension. All the questions she'd planned to ask evaporated, leaving nothing but a hollow feeling of betrayal in her chest. When she finally gathered the courage to look her sister in the eye, she found a complex expression of resignation, regret, and something else. Something that appeared unsettlingly like relief.

Ophelia sank to her knees. "I've dreaded and hoped for this day in equal measure. I suppose we have rather a lot to talk about."

CHAPTER 20

Confessions

Imogen opened her mouth to speak, but still no words came. Her mind kept circling back to all the little oddities over the years that suddenly made terrible sense – the unexpected skills, the strange phone calls to anonymous people, the doors that opened, the knack for coded messages. How many of their conversations had been built on lies? How many of her sister's stories were fabrications?

"You're a spy," she finally managed to croak.

Ophelia sank onto the side of the bed, the ancient springs creaking in protest. "Was. I *was* a spy." She reached for her sister's hand, but Imogen snatched it back in a reflex motion.

"Come on, ducky. I never killed anyone."

"But you lied to me. To mother."

"It's kind of the definition of a spy, wouldn't you agree?"

Outside, the sound of car engines drifted up from the street, a jarring reminder of the normal world continuing on while their private one had moved beneath their feet.

Imogen touched the photograph of Pierre. "I sensed that you and he had a history, even hinted at it, but you kept it from me."

Ophelia pointed to the wallet. "That license you're holding prevented me from telling anyone anything. I had to swear on the bible and to the Crown that I would not reveal my undercover function for the government to anyone. Even you. The penalty was death for treason. Do you understand?"

Imogen's expression clouded. "Will you get into trouble now?"

"No. *You* won't tell anyone, and I'm no longer on active duty." Ophelia pinched the bridge of her nose and Imogen witnessed a fraction of just what her sister's secret burden had cost.

She felt her anger wane. "Is this ring real?"

"Real enough but not representative of an actual marriage. I wouldn't keep something that significant from you, whatever they made me promise. I wore it on some of my undercover missions."

"How did it all begin?" Imogen asked, absently tracing the edges of the license.

Ophelia hesitated, the rejection from moments before still stinging. Her clandestine past lay scattered, each object a brick in the invisible wall that had formed between them.

Imogen found herself reaching for her sister's hand – the same gesture of reconciliation she had rejected moments before. Ophelia squeezed her fingers, accepting her sister's olive leaf, thankful for the invitation to explain and reconcile. It might not be total forgiveness yet, but it was a start.

"I was recruited. Like Evelyn and Ralph from the book club case. I was single, lived alone, traveled the continent with the orchestra, and I flatter myself that I was reasonably intelligent. I ticked all the right boxes."

She lifted the wedding ring, turning it in circles with her fingers. "I know it's a shock. But it was important work." She stared into Imogen's eyes. "I made a difference."

"What did you actually do?"

Ophelia reacted automatically, miming the familiar motion of opening her violin case. "It all started off very simply. Someone would leave me a coded message in a pre-arranged drop location, and I would hide the missive in the lining of my instrument case. After our performance, people would gather to meet us at the back door. Among them would be another agent.

We communicated through covert code phrases. Once I was satisfied the person was a friend, I slipped them the message. Or vice versa. In that case, I would decode the missive in the privacy of my hotel room and memorize it before destroying the paper. Straightforward. No danger."

Imogen tried to wrap her head around it all. "Like in the novels."

"It was rather," Ophelia agreed.

"When did it change?"

Ophelia leaned back on her elbows. "In the run up to the war. Tensions were rising. Spies were being unveiled. The stakes were much higher. But the orchestra continued performing in France, Germany, Italy and Spain. And no one would suspect a middle-aged spinster of espionage. I was an obvious choice for more difficult tasks like taking photographs. If you fish in the bottom of that box, there's a flower pendant. It's actually a tiny camera."

Their whole relationship suddenly felt like a carefully constructed piece of theater. "I'm sorry, it's just a lot to take in."

"I know. My oath to Crown and country sealed my silence, even from you. The secrets I kept weren't mine to share." She grabbed her sister by the arms. "But it was thrilling, don't you see? The intelligence I gathered helped prepare us for what was coming. Lives depended on my work … and on my silence. When war clouds were gathering, I was one of many working in the shadows to protect what mattered most." Ophelia let Imogen process this for a while.

While she'd been raising her children in the safety of the countryside, Ophelia had been caught in a web of international intrigue. She still could not believe that her brilliant, musical sister had been living a double life. What would her parents have said? "How did you meet Pierre?"

Ophelia stood and crossed to the window, her reflection ghostly in the darkening glass. "He was one of my contacts in Paris. Though he lived in England it did not raise eyebrows for him to travel to France regularly. Plus, he could always say he was chasing antiques for his business. He'd occasionally attend the concert then meet me at the back door with the other fans." She pivoted to face her sister. "We felt an immediate connection and I was always disappointed if another agent was sent. But acting on our feelings would have been insanity – not to mention it was expressly forbidden."

A cart clattered past on the street below.

"Did *he* end up doing more dangerous things?"

"Oh, yes. Since he spoke both English and French fluently, Pierre was an invaluable resource immediately before the war. Each assignment could have been his last." She paced as she spoke, her shadow moving across the wall like a second self.

"Did he work for the French government or the British?"

A gust of wind rattled the old windowpanes reminding them that it was winter outside.

"British. But since we were allies, what he did for us helped his mother country."

Imogen was reluctant to ask the next question that came to mind, but Ophelia must have seen it in her eyes. "You want to know if we fell in love?"

"Did you?" She twisted her own wedding ring.

"As I said, it was absolutely prohibited, but it turns out you cannot regulate matters of the heart. Pierre was older than me, but we were both seasoned agents, mature enough to understand the risks. Against our better judgment, we did allow a fondness to develop between us."

Even now, over a decade later, the memory of their stolen moments together made her chest ache. How could she explain that their shared danger had made every moment together more vivid, more precious?

She plucked the photograph of them outside the coliseum from the ground, touching its edges, stopping at the creased corner and remembering the scorching Roman summer day when it was taken. They had been tracking a German courier, playing their roles as besotted tourists so convincingly that a passing Italian had insisted on capturing their 'honeymoon' moment. Pierre had started to refuse – it was against the rules to leave a trace – but something in the genuine happiness of the moment had made him pause. He'd whispered, "After all we've been through, I think we deserve a piece of truth among all the lies." The next day, everything had gone wrong, and she had cherished this memory of that one moment of pure joy.

But now her sister was waiting.

"When the war began and Pierre's missions became more dangerous, he couldn't bear the thought of me suffering, as he had after losing his fiancée years before. So, we ended it – if what we had could even be called a real beginning. And oh, how I cried!"

Her sister and Pierre had been in love! Imogen's throat tightened, these glimpses of her sister's hidden joy and pain too much to bear. She wept inside for all the things she did not know, all the life experiences she had not been able to share with her twin. "Oh, lovey! What a tortured love life you've led. I feel so lucky to have met steady Wilf."

Ophelia smiled. "Wilf was an amazing man. I don't mind confessing I was rather jealous of your bliss. But as I've said before, I relished my life. If I'd married, it would all have come to a crashing end; the orchestra, the travel, and the danger." She smoothed the photograph against her chest. "Years later, when Pierre decided to relocate his business to Saffron Weald, I knew it was no accident, no matter what he claimed. Mother and I would browse his store, and though I tried to act normal, her shrewd eyes missed nothing. She recognized the weight of our unspoken history. I believe that's another reason she wanted me to move to Saffron Weald after retirement, to let us have a second chance."

Imogen had to admit, Mrs. Harrington had a sixth sense about these things. "Mother always was very sensitive to matters of the heart."

An image wandered across Ophelia's mind of Pierre helping her mother into the store or carrying her purchases all the way to Badger's Hollow. "Pierre treated her with extra care. She responded to that special attention."

Imogen shrugged. "Pierre treats everyone like that."

"It's true. But with Mother it was more pronounced."

For the first time since discovering the confidential information, Imogen saw past the hurt, to the ill-fated love story buried in the documents. The question that had burned on her tongue for months, that she had never dared ask, spilled out. "Are you still in love? I try not to pry, but I've wanted to know for so long."

Ophelia gripped her sister by the shoulders. "Yes! Mother's plan worked. With nothing keeping us apart, we are more in love than ever."

They danced around the room like a couple of children.

"This is wonderful news. Are you going to marry?"

"We are, but there's a slight problem."

"Not more red tape?"

"No, nothing like that. You know the ring that was stolen from Pierre's shop?"

"Yes!"

"It was to be my engagement ring."

"How cruel!"

Ophelia felt her eyes shining. "It doesn't matter. We can find another ring."

"Oh, my darling girl! I'm so delighted for you both, lovey. Ecstatic!"

They collapsed onto the bed, their energy spent.

"And you need have no fear about being alone. I will insist Pierre comes to live with us at Badger's Hollow—unless you object?"

Imogen raised both hands in surrender. "No objection from me. I think it's a *wonderful* idea." She had a thought. "When did you retire from being a secret agent?"

"1925. The war and its fallout were over, and the government hoped such a worldwide conflict would never happen again. Older people like me were let go. They still have spies of course, but they're a new batch, younger and more intelligent. They recruit them from universities, I hear."

The metal box sat below them, its contents still strewn across the floor.

"My sister, the spy. Unfathomable."

Though years of Ophelia's double-life had finally been unveiled, Imogen knew there were still depths to her sister she might never fully understand. As she helped Ophelia gather the treasures, she observed her with new eyes. Her twin, her closest friend, now somehow a stranger yet more familiar than ever.

CHAPTER 21

Victorian Mercy

The iconic, Georgian townhouse gleamed in the early spring sunlight. Elaborate, curlicue, wrought-iron window boxes – empty now but holding the promise of colorful blooms in the warmer months – graced each floor. Imogen could almost hear the distant echo of Victorian era servants' shoes scuffing down the stone stairs to the basement kitchen, the housekeeper making life miserable for the scullery maids, the pompous butler directing the footman upstairs.

As the twins prepared to knock, they had no idea if the mother of the deceased soldier Judith had treated, still lived here. But this was the address listed in the soldier's records.

The grand front door was opened by a tall woman dressed in black, a set of keys dangling from her pocket. How times had changed.

"May I help you?" she asked, barely concealing her astonishment at the sight of the identical older women on her doorstep.

"We're not sure," confessed Imogen. "We're in search of a Mrs. Moneymaker."

The housekeeper nodded. "That is my mistress. May I ask what this is about?"

Ophelia spoke. "We recently learned of the death of her son during the war because it may be connected to an incident that occurred in Meadowshire a few days ago."

The woman frowned. "Mr. Arthur Moneymaker has been gone for over a decade. How can anything concerning him possibly be connected to something that happened now?"

Imogen dropped her voice while Ophelia glanced around to make sure no one was listening. "We believe the connection may be through his *child*."

Now they had her attention. The woman's expression evolved from a mixture of curiosity and disdain to horrified concern. In a hoarse whisper, she asked, "How in the world could this relate to Master Sebastian?" She moved as if to close the door.

Ophelia decided that pussyfooting politeness was not helping their cause. "We may appear to be idle meddlers at first glance, but I can assure you we have been endowed with authority from the Meadowshire police. If you doubt us, please call Inspector Southam of Parkford. We'll wait." It was a bluff, though she offered the housekeeper the inspector's card. She had stretched the truth, but Judith's life might depend upon their meeting with Mrs. Moneymaker.

"It is *imperative* we speak with your mistress. Her information may help prevent the murder of an innocent woman, a woman we might add, who tended to Sergeant Moneymaker in his last moments." This at least was entirely honest.

The stern housekeeper glared. "Look here! Don't try to play on my emotions by mentioning Mr. Moneymaker. I don't know what you really want but it's my job to protect the mistress from charlatans like you. Now, if you don't mind." Her hands caught the edge of the door.

"If Mrs. Moneymaker won't talk to us, she may be forced to speak with the authorities which might invite undue attention," blurted out Imogen.

The door stopped in its progress. "You really are with the police? Since when do they employ elderly women?"

The insult plunged into Ophelia's chest like a knife. *I am* not *that old!*

Sensing the rise in her sister's blood pressure, Imogen jumped in. "I can assure you we are not charlatans. We're on an errand to help a country headmistress who was recently poisoned. If you don't believe us, call Inspector Southam." She directed her gaze to the card in the housekeeper's hand.

A war was waging behind the woman's sharp eyes. "Wait here."

"Do you think she'll see us?" asked Imogen as they watched cars and carriages rattle by. A milkman was delivering his wares to a basement across the street, and a car backfired, scattering a flock of pigeons from a nearby roof.

Ophelia chewed her cheek, still smarting from the housekeeper's comment. "I'd say we have a fifty-fifty chance."

The stern woman returned. "Mrs. Moneymaker will see you, but only for ten minutes."

Black and white tile gleamed in the sunlight and a curved staircase led to an upper level. They followed the testy housekeeper down a corridor where she opened a door, standing back to let them pass. Ophelia noted the fact that there was no butler and no footmen.

Inside the room sat a dainty woman about the same age as themselves. Her beautifully styled, gray hair rose from her forehead and ended in a tidy roll at the base of her neck. A diamond hair clip twinkled in the light from the window. She seemed to melt into her surroundings, her lavender dress almost indistinguishable from the room's lavender haze.

Feet resting on a plush footstool, Mrs. Moneymaker stroked the fur of a pretty tabby cat, concern stamped on her brow as her eyes jumped from one face to another. The feline opened one eye to assess the visitors, then resumed its contented dozing. Sheet music scattered across the grand piano hinted that their call had interrupted her morning practice.

"Do sit down." Each syllable was crafted with the careful precision of old money.

The twins complied, backs rigid, on the edge of a feminine,

silk settee, handbags primly on their knees.

"Now what is this all about? My housekeeper said a nurse who attended my son may be murdered?"

No customary small talk. Their low rank did not demand it.

Ophelia explained the connection of her grandchild's mother to their headmistress.

Mrs. Moneymaker did not respond right away. She fondled the cat and dipped her chin, her mind spinning behind active eyes.

Imogen appreciated how many social rules this Victorian grandmother had broken, simply by admitting to the existence of an illegitimate grandchild. It struck her as remarkably brave.

Mrs. Moneymaker lifted the spoiled cat to her cheek. "You think that Sebastian's mother may be involved with this poisoning? I'm afraid I have to tell you that you are laboring under a misapprehension. Madeleine died of the Spanish influenza in 1918 when the boy was just a baby."

"Oh," said both twins together. Ophelia scolded herself; they should have done some investigating at St. Catherine's House. It might have saved them a trip.

Mrs. Moneymaker rang a small bell that stood on an occasional table by her chair. "Let's have some tea."

Obviously, in spite of this misstep, the twins had passed some kind of test.

A slip of a maid appeared, drowning in her oversized black and white uniform, the lace bandeau threatening to slip over one eye. Ophelia realized the girl had been stationed outside the drawing room.

After the maid retired, Mrs. Moneymaker pointed a finger at the twins. "Which one of you played violin for the Queen's Orchestra?"

"That was me," replied Ophelia, realizing this was why they had been invited to stay after the completion of their business. "I retired last year."

"Yes, I wondered where you'd gone. I'm a patron of that orchestra." She gestured to the piano. "As a fellow musician, I feel it important to support the arts, though I do not claim the proficiency level achieved during *your* professional career. What was it like, being free to be independent and travel the world?"

Ophelia's eyes lit up with remembered adventures. "Though my life has been unconventional, I would not change a thing. I have lived exactly the life I wanted – on my own terms."

Imogen could not help remembering the revelations from the night before. Mirror images of each other from birth, they had carved out entirely different lives – one finding joy in motherhood and village life, the other in concert halls and secret missions. Yet each had created her own kind of happiness and neither sister would have traded places with the other.

"My music took me to locations I had never dreamed of seeing. Every city, every concert hall held a new possibility. I wouldn't change a moment."

A wistful energy animated Mrs. Moneymaker's features. "There are so many more opportunities for women in this day and age. That's why it is so hard to find servants. They can earn more working in a factory or in a shop *and* have their independence."

The maid returned with a silver tray and tea pot.

"And you my dear," she said, addressing Imogen. "Are you a musician too?"

"No. I play the piano reasonably well, but I followed the traditional route of wife and motherhood. My husband died two years ago."

The maid poured as Mrs. Moneymaker offered her condolences. "I'm so sorry. I'm a widow myself. Thank you, Brown. That will do."

The tiny maid curtsied and left once more.

"Now that we're alone, I can admit that your coming here today has peaked my interest. I had no idea that Sebastian's mother had persecuted your friend, but knowing her as I do, I am not totally surprised. She was always a little unstable. She trapped my son, you know."

Ophelia's hackles rose. Both parties should take equal responsibility in situations such as this, but in her experience, it was often the man who was actually at fault. She took a sip of tea to prevent herself from saying something she might regret.

Imogen noticed Ophelia's shoulders stiffen and the slight tilt of her head, subtle gestures that together spoke volumes to her twin who recognized her sister's carefully controlled disagreement.

"The war took so many of our best and brightest young men. Your son and others like him died defending this great country, but it was the wives and mothers who bore much of that cost. No mother should have to bear such news."

Mrs. Moneymaker's expression softened. "Did you lose anyone?"

"I was one of the lucky ones," responded Imogen. "My son came home a little worse for wear but with no permanent damage done. We were most fortunate."

They allowed their host to reminisce for some time.

"Judith Rutherford, the nurse, said your son was in bad shape when he arrived at the hospital."

Mrs. Moneymaker gave the barest hint of assent, though her eyes began to shine. "That is my understanding too. There was nothing anyone could have done."

Ophelia decided to take a risk. "Did you know about Madeleine at the time?"

As intended, the direct question took Mrs. Moneymaker off guard, the teacup hovering halfway to her lips. "No! It was the greatest shock, especially to my husband. She arrived on our doorstep one day, obviously in the family way, demanding that we support her and the baby." Her gaze wandered to a picture on the piano of a handsome young man in full military dress. "As you may imagine, my husband threw her out. Told her never to darken our doorstep again." A flash of old pain crossed her features. "But she was carrying *my* grandchild. Arthur was my only child, so with his death came the realization that I would never have the joy of grandchildren. Though I was in deep mourning for my son, Madeleine's arrival changed my future. My husband would not understand." The cat began a deep throated purr. "I sent my maid after Madeleine with a five-pound note, asking for her address. I defied my husband and supported her and the child, behind his back, until her death from the influenza in 1918." She paused, considering the past. "Her own family had disowned her. I ensured she was cared for during her sickness, and after she died, I hired a nurse for the baby and found them decent lodging nearby. As soon as my husband passed away, I took the child in as my ward." The admission brought a touch of pink to her cheeks, but her chin lifted with a defiance that suggested she would make the same decision again.

"What you did was remarkably brave," Imogen said softly.

"Not many would have had the courage," added Ophelia, changing her mind about the woman.

Mrs. Moneymaker fluttered a lacy handkerchief. "He's eleven now and in his first year at Rugby Boarding School." She indicated a framed photograph of a fine-looking adolescent in cricket whites. "I miss him so much. He looks just like his father which soothes my aching heart. That was taken just last term. He's already made the junior cricket team, just as his father did." Pride softened her aristocratic features. "Of course, the other boys don't know about his ... circumstances. As far as they're concerned, he is my grandson from my late son's marriage. It's better that way."

The cat stretched and resettled as she continued. "He's to come home for the Easter holidays next month and I can hardly wait." Her voice trailed off, and she seemed to remember she was speaking to strangers. "But I'm sure you don't want to hear an old woman ramble on about her grandson."

"I quite understand," responded Imogen. "I have grandchildren of my own. I'm happy that things have worked out for you." She grabbed her gloves and moved to the edge of the settee. "We shan't take any more of your time."

Ophelia followed her lead.

"Sebastian has brought such joy and purpose to my old age. And I am grateful to have no fear that he will be called on to be a soldier since the Great War was called the war to end all wars." She rang the bell again. "It has been a pleasure meeting both of you."

🎭

"Did Mrs. Moneymaker make you angry?" asked Imogen as they left the house.

"A little. But she's merely a product of her time and status. And I have to admit that she rose in my estimation when I learned she had supported the girl and taken in the baby. Honestly, it's more than most people would do, even today."

"It's true. She risked being ostracized by society."

They navigated the busy street, dodging a delivery boy on his bicycle. "And now we know that this line of inquiry is a dead end, we can turn our attention to comrade Martov."

Imogen winced. "He sounds dangerous. Don't you think we should leave him to the police?"

"I shall give all the relevant information to Inspector Southam, but if Martov's been hiding out in Saffron Weald in the dead of winter, I think there might be evidence of the fact. Personally, I'm eager to poke around places he could hide looking for traces of his presence."

They found a bus stop that would take them close to Ophelia's apartment. A thin drizzle had started to fall, and Ophelia opened her umbrella, holding it so they could both shelter beneath its protection.

Imogen stuck her arm out as a bus approached. "You mean like the abandoned cottage?" The wheels of the bus sent up spray from the wet street as it pulled into the curb. They both jumped out of the way before boarding the bus.

"Yes, and people's outbuildings." Ophelia paused, watching an elegant couple hurry past under a shared umbrella, making her think of Pierre. "Someone staying in the village through the winter months would need food, water, warmth. There'd be evidence of their existence."

The bus lurched forward and they each grabbed a silver pole before sliding onto a damp bench seat.

"Tiger can help us with that. He has a super smeller. Though I must say, the idea of hunting a murderous Russian revolutionary, even with the dog to protect us, makes my knees go wobbly." Imogen glanced out the rain-streaked window as the grand mansions gave way to more modest homes. "What if we manage to find him?"

Ophelia's expression hardened "We'll need to be very careful he doesn't find us first. Men like him, don't leave witnesses."

CHAPTER 22

Red Dresses and Red Herrings

They were all on their second helping of apple pie and rich, creamy custard. Pierre loosened his belt, sighing with contentment. "You ladies would not be out of your league in France. This is delicious."

Ophelia swiped him with a handy tea towel. "Why do the French always have to criticize English cuisine?"

He gestured with both palms. "You 'ave to admit, not everyone in England is as gifted in the kitchen as you, chérie."

They had spent the whole of dinner telling Pierre about their trip to London and Imogen's discovery of Ophelia's clandestine past.

"My sister is curious to know if you've ever had to kill anyone?"

Imogen felt heat rush to her cheeks.

Pierre's jaw resisted a smile. "Some things are better left unsaid."

Trust your sister to land you right in it!

It was time to steer the conversation away from her. "Ophelia also told me you'd picked out a ring for a proposal and that it was the one that was stolen."

"Yes. Most frustrating." Pierre folded his arms. "I'm beginning to think it was just a common or garden shoplifter."

"Is that so?" Ophelia felt a punch of disappointment. "Then you may never get it back."

He took her hand. "It is the person who is irreplaceable, not the ring."

Though Ophelia was not one to wear a great deal of jewelry, she *had* set her heart on the stunning ring.

He pushed up her chin with his finger. "I shall find you a more spectacular one, chérie."

To cover her chagrin, Ophelia asked, "Speaking of thieves, did you catch anyone trying to retrieve the key from the automaton clock?"

"Not yet. I'm afraid our clever idea of a trap 'as failed."

"Perhaps we just need to be more patient."

"I think my presence might be a deterrent, and since I 'ave upgraded my locks and employ Tiger as a security guard, the person who left it, cannot break in to retrieve the key from the clock." He chucked his chin. "What we need is for some movie director to set up an 'idden camera. Haha! What am I saying? That is ridiculous."

Imogen was far less interested in the key than her sister's nuptials. "When are you thinking of getting married?"

Pierre and Ophelia locked eyes.

"We haven't discussed dates yet," admitted her sister, meeting Pierre's gaze. "And I have yet to inform him that we're a matched set and one of the conditions is that he must come to live here in the cottage once we marry."

Pierre rocked back on his chair with that winsome smile that made any female weak at the knees. "Don't worry. I 'ad already figured that one out. But I will insist on redecorating this kitchen." He gestured to the eclectic room with his arm.

The sisters laughed. It was on their list of things to do but they had been so busy solving cases, leading the church choir, assisting the amateur dramatics society and reading for the book club, that they had not got around to it.

Ophelia kissed him right on the mouth. "With our blessing."

The conversation fell into a lull as they finished their pie and Imogen decided it was the perfect opportunity to be nosy.

Holding her empty bowl for Tiger to lick, she asked, "Pierre, tell me when you first began to have feelings for my sister."

The deep throaty laugh they were well used to, bubbled out of his mouth. "I don't think I 'ave ever told anyone this." He reached for Ophelia's hand. "Not even you!" He brought her knuckles to his lips. "I 'ad been undercover for about two years when I was told to meet a new recruit in Paris at the Théâtre Du Châtelet. I was informed she was a violinist with the British orchestra performing there, and that I was to meet 'er at the back door, where admirers congregated. 'Er mission was to pass me a coded message. As a lover of the symphony, I was thrilled.

"During the performance, one particular musician caught my eye. 'Er 'air was the color of wheat then and I found myself mesmerized. She became one with the violin and I was entranced. Of course, I 'ad no idea she was the spy I was supposed to make contact with.

"Imagine my surprise when this vision exited the theatre, 'er gown flowing like the reflection of the moon on water. After graciously greeting all 'er admirers, she glided over to me and casually asked if I liked my bacon fried or boiled. This was the code phrase. I nearly fumbled the drop—I was too distracted by the elegant curve of her neck and the classical beauty of her features."

"I had no idea," responded Ophelia, a blush on her cheek. "I was incredibly nervous. It was my first assignment."

"I could not stop thinking about you, chérie. I tried to find out where you lived in London but my 'andler forbade it. You must know that most female spies were rather plain. I 'oped and prayed that you would be my contact on my next assignment, but a whole year passed before we met again. Do you remember?"

Imogen was fascinated by the light in her sister's eyes.

"Vividly. You asked me to dinner that night, and I refused. My training had drummed into me that romantic entanglements between agents was cause for termination and a deadly risk."

"It was Nice, you remember? A beautiful city, for a beautiful woman. You 'ad three more performances and I attended all of them, waiting by the back door like a lovesick puppy. But you never came out."

Remember? Her memory of Nice was vivid. She'd had trouble staying focused on her music during the concerts that followed, knowing that Pierre was somewhere in the audience, but she suspected that her handler might be in attendance too.

"I was sorely tempted."

Everything sounded impossibly exotic and exciting to Imogen.

"Over the next two years, we crossed paths several times. I tried to rein in my feelings, but it got 'arder and 'arder until that fateful night in Vienna. Your assignment was to photograph documents in the Russian ambassador's study, while I kept 'im busy at the embassy reception. But when I saw you in that red dress..." Pierre's voice trailed off. "Then I noticed that the guards were making their rounds earlier than usual and I panicked."

Ophelia's hand tightened on his as the memory washed over her. The whisper of satin against her legs, the ruby flower pendant. The agency had spared no expense on the gown, ensuring she would blend seamlessly with the diplomatic elite.

"You almost blew your cover to come and warn me."

Pierre's face darkened. "The guards 'ad switched their rotation schedule without warning and were 'eaded for the study. It was impossible for Ophelia to 'ave completed her mission in so short a time. I 'ad to prevent her from being caught red-'anded." He shook his head. "Protocol demanded I maintain my cover, but I could not bear the thought of Ophelia being captured. They would 'ave shot her on the spot."

Imogen's hands flew to her mouth. Suddenly, espionage did not sound at all glamorous.

"It's true. You helped me hide in a closet and started a fire in the cloakroom."

"Not my finest moment," he admitted with a wry smile. "But

I 'ad no time to think and it did succeed in getting everyone out of the embassy, including you with the film." His thumb traced circles on her palm. "That was the night you kissed me—not a passionate kiss but a bisou, a peck on the cheek, for saving you. I didn't wash my face for a month." His expression softened, then grew pained. "And that night I knew it must stop, that my infatuation could get us both killed. The cruel irony was that you chose that same night to finally let your guard down." Pierre's voice grew hoarse. "Your coded message arrived at my 'otel near dawn – just three lines that changed my whole world. Following years of keeping your distance, you were finally ready to risk it all. But I..." He squeezed her hand. "I 'ad already made my choice. I could not bear to be the reason you were captured, tortured, or killed. Better to break both our 'earts than to lead you into mortal danger."

Pierre ran a finger along her cheek. "Therefore, I did the 'ardest thing I ever 'ad to do. I told you that it could not be. You know not 'ow much that 'urt me."

Memories poured into Ophelia's mind. He was right. The thrill, the excitement, the electricity between them, had all come to a head for her that night and she had thrown caution to the wind.

Though earlier that very day, in the home of Mrs. Moneymaker, she had claimed no regrets, Ophelia had been ready to surrender to her feelings in Vienna and declare her love for Pierre. His return note had shattered her heart into a million pieces.

Ophelia wrapped their hands together. "I cried myself to sleep that night and many others. The handlers must have sensed that something had shifted between us. They kept us apart for months. Different countries, different missions."

Pierre's face filled with blissful triumph. "But fate 'ad other plans, n'est-ce pas? I could not forget you, could not stop myself from searching. Then, by chance, I discovered where your parents lived." A gleam of mischief crossed his face. "It took some doing to arrange everything, but within six months I 'ad moved my business to Saffron Weald. And now..." He brushed another kiss across her knuckles. "Now we are both free from the shadows, free to write the ending of our own story."

Imogen wiped her eyes, lips trembling. "What a beautiful, tragic story."

The trio sat in silence for a moment, the weight of past sacrifices causing deep reflection. Finally, Pierre cleared his throat, turning to matters of the present. "Alors, 'ave you told Judith the bad news about Martov?"

"Fortunately, she's still in the county hospital. We'll take a trip out there tomorrow. We can also tell her that Sebastian Moneymaker is thriving."

The sun made a valiant attempt at appearing through the clouds the following morning, and since the newspaper stated there was no rain in the forecast, the twins postponed their trip to Parkford in favor of scouring the village for signs of someone sleeping rough. The most obvious place to start was the abandoned cottage.

Winter had stripped away the building's riotous summer disguise. Where dense foliage had once hidden the ruins from view, bare branches now reached around the walls like a prickly hug and out of the windows like witches' bony fingers, the naked boughs and twigs exposing the building's decay. Through shattered windowpanes, undisturbed dust painted every surface in ghostly gray, thick enough to prove that no footsteps had disturbed this sanctuary in recent memory.

Tiger bounded ahead through the tangled weeds, tail high, nose low. The sisters followed his meandering path around the cottage, watching as he stopped to investigate each new scent. Despite enthusiastic exploration of burrow holes and bramble patches, he showed none of the tension that would signal human presence. Only the wild residents of the abandoned property had left their marks here – rabbits, foxes, and the occasional badger.

With no signs of life at the cottage, they moved on to check the outlying properties around the village, focusing on houses with outbuildings. Having obtained permission from each homeowner, they began their systematic search.

The first outbuilding, a sturdy stone barn that housed a large tractor and a great deal of wandering chickens, caused Imogen to worry that the dog might attack them. To her relief, Tiger was surprisingly gentle with the birds. He carefully surveyed every corner of the stone structure, but even after twenty minutes of unbridled sniffing, he had not uncovered the existence of a stranger bedding down for the night.

A quarter mile down the lane, they came to their next target: a stable block built of the same materials as the village houses. Inside, several horses watched curiously as Tiger searched the fresh hay in their stalls. A quick look disclosed no unexpected guests, though they did have trouble convincing Tiger to abandon his new friends.

Arriving at their next quarry necessitated a brisk march across Farmer Whitby's south field. Halfway through, Ophelia froze, pointing to a curl of smoke from the other side of a tall hedgerow. Tipping her head in that direction to apprise Imogen, the sisters put Tiger back on the lead and stalked over. Falling silent, they searched for a gap in the dense hedge that towered above them. Finding one, Imogen gestured frantically to Ophelia. Peering through the scratchy hole, they observed the remains of a small fire and an area of flattened grass.

"Bingo! Someone was here but they've moved on," declared Imogen.

"I don't see any evidence that it was Martov and not some random vagrant," warned Ophelia. "I suggest we look for clues and let Tiger become familiar with the scent."

The hedge was far too high and thorny to climb, forcing them to trek a mile around its perimeter to reach the other side. A morning of trudging across the countryside had rendered their legs heavy, and their enthusiasm was waning. Only Tiger seemed undaunted, pulling eagerly at his lead until Imogen produced treats from her pocket to calm him.

Finally arriving at the smoldering embers of the fire, they poked through the ash and carefully examined the vegetation surrounding it. Within a few minutes, Tiger nosed out some spent cigarettes crushed under the flattened grass. Ophelia held one to her nose and quickly deduced that it was the same brand she had found outside the church hall the night Kitty had been accosted by her former beau, Jack Scroggins. She had assumed the cigarettes were Jack's, but now she had to consider that there may have been *two* men outside the village hall that night, possibly *three* if she counted Bob Sugden.

Tiger explored the periphery of the fire then fixed on a portion of the hedge. Noticing something, Imogen pulled out a crumpled wrapper with a blue stamp containing remnants of meat fat.

"That's *Cleaver's* butcher paper," remarked Ophelia. "Whoever slept here, searched the bins behind the shops for scraps."

The hair on the back of Ophelia's neck prickled. Tiger lifted his snout and sniffed the air. Ophelia looked around. Could she feel someone watching them? She checked the dog's demeanor again. No. It was a case of overwrought nerves, nothing more.

She returned her attention to the fire. If this was Martov, he was a man on the run and would choose a different spot each night to avoid detection. What was his end game? Why was he here? And if he was in the vicinity, why had he not made contact with Judith? Or was it Martov that had tried to kill her? If so, what was his motive? Wasn't she his friend? If he had struck out, in case she recognized him and turned him in to the police, why come to Saffron Weald in the first place? There were so many questions.

"I know this is not definitive, but I think we should call Inspector Southam before we head to the hospital. I believe he'll agree this encampment is suspicious enough for him to assign more resources to the problem."

Imogen stood arms akimbo, regarding the field around them. "I'm very happy to hear you say that, lovey, because my feet are complaining and I need a rest."

"Good afternoon, Inspector. This is Miss Harrington. My sister and I have been quite busy and have some interesting updates for you."

A strange sound like a cross between exasperation and admiration came through the line. "Let's hear it then."

Ophelia first chronicled their trip to London, their visit to Whitehall and their discovery that the writer of the nasty letters had been dead for some years. Then she brought him up to date on their recent discovery of someone sleeping rough in Saffron Weald.

The inspector growled. "How come my men didn't think of this?"

"In their defense, they didn't know about the elusive Russian."

"Mmmm, I suppose so. It's always good when we can completely eliminate someone from our inquiries." He snorted. "But this Martov, fellow. How dangerous do you think he is?"

"Let's put it this way, Inspector. We saw a heavily redacted version of his thick dossier and it was clear that people in his orbit disappeared, never to be seen again."

The inspector choked. "Are you saying he should be considered armed and dangerous?"

"I don't think that would be exaggerating the case. If he *is* hiding out in Saffron Weald, as we suspect, it puts every villager in danger. I think you will agree that we should consider it our duty to alert the population, at this point."

"Right. What do you propose? Fliers?"

Ophelia huffed. "I believe there's a much more efficient way, Inspector. We'll just tell Mildred Chumbley and the whole village will be on alert in five minutes flat."

The inspector chuckled. "The old village grapevine. Excellent idea. I'll direct the extra uniforms in Saffron Weald to be on the alert and we'll cast a net around the village, so to speak. We'll soon catch the fellow."

"I can't say with one hundred percent certainty that Martov's here but given his character I'd say it was better to be safe than sorry."

"Indeed."

"I don't know if this will help but we also found old cigarettes by the fire. Just like the ones outside the village hall before the murder. Did you ever match the one we found on the stage to that brand?"

"We did. Those found outside and the one on the stage were the same, but I'm afraid it's not a strong clue since so many people smoke these days."

"Yes, I thought that might be the case." An idea sparked in her head. "Since we do fear Martov to be in the area, may I also suggest putting a policeman outside Judith's hospital ward?"

She heard a grumbling sound. "You think she's still in danger? You believe he's the killer?"

"Honestly, logic is telling me that he has no motive to kill Judith, Inspector. He's fleeing from several international agencies as well as the British government, who are very interested in his capture. Furthermore, Judith was his friend. Why come here to kill her? It doesn't make sense. Unless, of course, the headmistress didn't tell us everything."

"The man sounds like an absolute lunatic who kills people without a second thought, in which case he may not *need* a motive. I'll do as you suggest and put a police officer outside her door."

"I don't suppose you have any information you could share with me, Inspector?"

She heard rustling papers. "We brought Bob Sugden in for questioning. He admits to hanging around the village and watching his brother's family, but he says he doesn't even know who Miss Rutherford is. He could be lying, of course. However, we can find no connection between them, so he may be telling the truth. And we canvased the people in the pub in Parkford, and he *was* there on the night in question. They remembered him because of his alarming appearance and his accent, plus he was flashing his money about and buying rounds. However, he didn't have an alibi for the day Miss Rutherford was poisoned. But the chap is massive and looks like a right thug. I can't help feeling someone would have noticed a bloke like that sneaking into the school in broad daylight."

Something about this statement tickled Ophelia's brain.

"We interrogated him about his cash flow," continued the inspector. "He buttoned up tight, but when I mentioned his time served for robbing the bank, he got wobbly. I warned him that we are actively pursuing that line of investigation and advised him not to leave Parkford. But with no access to the stolen notes, I had to let him go. I'm going to see if the pub still has the money and check the serial numbers against those that were stolen. I've put a tail on him. If Sugden tries to flee, we'll clap him in jail."

If the black sheep of the Sugden family was busy trying to keep the police from confiscating his ill-gotten gains, he would have less time to mess with Molly and her family. "That is excellent news, Inspector. Have you had the same luck with Jack Scroggins?"

The inspector's sigh carried the weight of mounting frustration. "That young man is a cocky so and so. Kitty is far better off without him. I told him to leave her be, let her start fresh after all her sorrows. He swears up and down he didn't set that fire, but I have my doubts. There's something about him— too smug by half, if you ask me. Claims he only came to Saffron Weald to persuade Kitty he's not a killer. Also maintains he was just as broken up about the fire as she was. I don't trust him as far as I could throw him."

"Hmmm. Sounds more like he can't take rejection, if you ask me. Do you have any evidence that he's running with a gang in Liverpool? Could be that one of the other gang members actually set the fire. That way he could claim innocence."

"I'm way ahead of you, Miss Harrington. I sent a telegram to the chief in Liverpool and he confirmed that Scroggins is a member of a gang. He looked up the file on the fire and by return telegram stated that it appears to have been started by a cigarette in the living room. There was no accelerant present which means it *could* have been an accident. However, Kitty's father smoked a pipe and no one else in the family smoked at all.

The case is still open."

Cigarettes again!

"Thank you, Inspector. You've been most helpful." Hanging up the phone, Ophelia sat heavily on the stairs, her mind buzzing. Three potential killers: a revolutionary on the run, a jilted lover with gang connections, and a bank robber trying to protect his freedom. And yet, after her enlightening conversation with the inspector, something still felt amiss.

The telephone's shrill ring gave her such a fright her heart nearly stopped. It was the hospital. Judith had regained consciousness and was asking for them.

As she grabbed her coat and called for Imogen, Ophelia could not banish the troubling impression they were missing something obvious. She did up the buttons one by one, still pondering, but as she reached for her hat, the fog of uncertainty lifted and her thoughts organized themselves into startling comprehension. All these potential suspects were complete *strangers* to the village. The killer had to be a person who knew Saffron Weald inside and out; someone familiar with the layout of fellowship hall, who had extensive knowledge of where the props were kept, be fully conversant with the time and dates of rehearsals. Furthermore, they had to be well acquainted with the floor plan of the school and schedule, intimate enough to be able to enter without attracting attention and know exactly when to strike ...

CHAPTER 23

Friend or Foe?

On the way to the hospital in Parkford, Ophelia filled Imogen in on her conversation with the inspector.

"All those strange men have been sneaking around Saffron Weald and Mildred Chumbley hasn't spotted any of them? She's losing a step." She chuckled. "But you're right. None of those shadowy fellows knows the place well enough to time their attacks as well as the murderer did. I'm surprised I didn't notice that discrepancy before. Even so, I must say I feel rather uncomfortable knowing a violent Russian revolutionary is hiding in the bushes."

"None of them are good men. At least two are already suspected of murder and the other went to prison for robbing a bank. Not really the sort of people we want loitering about in our quiet village."

Imogen watched the countryside speed by from her seat in the back of the bus. "Indeed." She sat silent for a moment pondering. "It does have to be a local then, doesn't it? Any ideas?"

"We're back to the people who were participating in the play. Alice took the wine glasses onto the stage. She had ample opportunity to slip poison into one of them."

"Are you seriously considering Alice Puddingfield as a

suspect?"

"Of course not! But I am trying to follow where the facts lead us. Anyone on that side of the stage could have introduced the poison into the glass." She pulled the notebook out of her handbag.

"Alice, Judith, Mildred, Patricia, Kitty, Molly and Celina were on that side. Plus, Prudence and Ed Sugden in the wings as stagehands."

The bus took a corner too quickly sending all the passengers sliding along their bench seats. Both the twins grabbed a pole and waited for the bus to straighten up. Imogen readjusted her hat.

"Well, we can take Judith off the list. She was the intended target. The second attempt was proof of that."

Ophelia tapped her lips. "Yeees."

"Are you thinking that the two events might not be connected?"

"Not really, but you're at a disadvantage when you automatically view the facts through one lens and ignore other possibilities, aren't you? What if Judith wasn't the intended target but she saw something and the killer wanted to silence her?"

"Now you're just making my head hurt," complained Imogen. "I'm going to consider them as two attempts on Judith's life until we have concrete evidence to the contrary."

The bus pulled up to a stop and an older couple got on and sat near them in the back.

"And *I'm* going to keep an open mind." Ophelia tapped her notebook with the pencil.

"I wonder why Judith wants to see us?" mused Imogen. "I mean we were going to visit her anyway, but still."

"Perhaps she *did* see something."

"In that case, why not call Inspector Southam instead of us? We can't really protect her."

The conductor approached and they both showed their return tickets.

Parkford hospital was on the edge of town set in a lovely park. Like *The Lion Hotel*, it had once been a manor house. When the noble family fell on hard times, the county purchased the property for a hospital. It dated from the late 1700s and was constructed using light colored brick. The facade featured ten windows upstairs and eight on the lower level with a huge double door entrance.

As they approached the reception desk, nurses crisscrossed their path, long white veils fluttering in the breeze behind them.

The sturdy bespectacled woman at the information desk raised her brows. "How can I help you?"

"We're here to see Miss Judith Rutherford," explained Imogen.

The receptionist glanced at the clock on the wall. "There's only half an hour of visiting time left."

"That's alright. We won't be long," Imogen assured her.

The officious woman ran a finger down the registration book. "Ward 6. Up the stairs and to the left."

Outside the ward door, stood a uniformed police officer. He held up a hand as if stopping traffic, his eyes darting between the twins. "This ward is not taking visitors."

"We're here to see Miss Rutherford. She called for us. You can check. I am Mrs. Pettigrew and this is my sister, Miss Harrington."

A nurse pushed open the swing door and the policeman stopped her. "Can you check the list for Miss Rutherford? This is …" he paused.

"Miss Harrington and Mrs. Pettigrew," said Ophelia.

The nurse pivoted, returning to the ward and two seconds later re-appeared. "They're cleared."

The ward held four female patients. Two were asleep. A shabbily dressed man sat beside the bed of Judith Rutherford. The twins gasped.

Mikhail Martov.

"It's alright," Judith assured them. "Mikhail is my friend."

Ophelia was certain Judith was being fooled. "This man has been living rough in Saffron Weald. Do you know his history? He's dangerous."

Mikhail made to get up from his chair, the look of a trapped rabbit on his gaunt face.

Judith reached out to touch his arm. "These are my friends. You have nothing to fear. I will explain everything."

Ophelia felt her pulse kick into flight mode. "Yes, please. Explain everything or we will call the policeman in."

Mikhail surrendered his chair to Imogen and fetched another for Ophelia. He stood by Judith's head. Her skin was ashen. Dark purple shadows smudged the skin under tired eyes and her thick hair lay flat against her head and around her shoulders.

The twins could not stop staring at the suspicious Russian.

"I'll have you know we've been to Whitehall and seen the file on this so-called friend of yours. He is a former comrade of Lenin and a suspect in many political assassinations."

Mikhail's shoulders slumped as he faced Judith. "You see how it is." Though his English was very good, the accent was thick as pea soup.

"You have it all wrong, Ophelia. Mikhail has told me everything. He was framed when he realized that Lenin was not the great benefactor he purported to be and ran away." Judith nodded to Mikhail.

"Before the October revolution, I admit I was a true disciple. I left teaching to become private secretary to one of Lenin's inner circle. The promises were intoxicating – peace for our soldiers, land for the peasants, bread for everyone. In the beginning, the excitement in the streets was electric. We truly believed we were building a better world for the poor."

His gaze grew distant. "But then came the first signs. Small things at first. The way certain people who asked difficult questions disappeared, how questioning even minor decisions became dangerous. I began keeping records, transcribing conversations, collecting documents. When there was no room for doubt that Lenin was a monster, I commissioned the creation of a small, portable, impenetrable safe, in the event I ever needed proof that I was not complicit in the rampant bloodshed. I made two keys for the safe, one I sewed into the lining of a bag I sent to my English friend Judith. She had no idea, you understand. The other I kept on a string around my neck." He grabbed his scruffy mustache.

"By 1918, the propaganda machine had turned against me. Suddenly I was branded a traitor, a saboteur, a foreign agent. They claimed I had murdered my own comrades. The night I planned to escape, they caught me, beat me, and ripped the key from my neck leaving me for dead. But I was not." He aimlessly fingered a deep scar that dragged his left eye down.

"For nine years, even after Lenin's death, I moved like a ghost through Europe, working as a laborer, a stable hand, anything to keep moving. Finally, I found peace in Brittany as a fisherman. Until..." He paused, his features darkening. "Until a comrade from the old country recognized me on the beach. Within hours, I was on a ferry to England. I knew I'd never have peace unless I could prove my innocence with those documents, and without that key I could not open the safe." His ragged clothes hung on his bony frame and every sentence seemed to drain his energy further.

"I came to Saffron Weald to find Judith and the other key," Mikhail continued. "But one night, as I watched her house from the shadows, I saw another figure lurking in the darkness. My old fears rushed back. Had the Stalinists found me after all these years? I couldn't risk falling into their hands, not after everything I'd sacrificed, not when I was so close to being able to prove my innocence. I retired to the anonymity of the countryside to try my luck another day." Wringing his hands he continued. "When I did finally manage to retrieve the key from Judith's bag, sewn into the lining of the gift I had sent her years before, I was still afraid that the presence I had felt outside her house was a spy from Russia. I needed somewhere to hide the key temporarily."

Judith sat up. "My bag! Remember? I mentioned the hole in it after the first rehearsal?"

Imogen recalled the offhand comment. "I do."

Mikhail hung his scrawny head. "I apologize. I felt hunted. There was no time to repair it. And I needed a place to hide the key quickly."

"The elephant clock," said Ophelia.

"Da! The antique shop seemed the perfect hiding place, people coming and going all day. I slipped in with a group of people dressed in rambling clothes so that I did not stand out too much, and hid the key inside the pretty clock sitting on the shelf. I planned to retrieve it once I was certain I was not being followed." His weathered face fell. "But when I returned the next day, the clock was gone."

"Did you steal a ring too?" asked Ophelia who was not convinced that this dirty, scruffy foreigner could be trusted.

Mikhail frowned in confusion. "I am many things – a fugitive, yes, perhaps even a coward – but I am not a thief. I do not steal. I merely hid the key in the clock, and now it is gone, and I cannot access the documents that will exonerate me."

Ophelia sighed and touched the chain at her neck. "I know where it is."

The despair in his expression vanished. "You do?"

"Yes, but I must insist you tell all this to Inspector Southam. Only then will I reveal the key's location."

His gaze slid to Judith, her face pale against the hospital pillow. "She's right. You'll have to trust the justice system to absolve you."

"And *I'm* not convinced you didn't try to kill Judith," said Imogen who had remained quiet during his story, her torso stiff with indignation. "Where were you the afternoon Judith was attacked at the school?"

He smiled and put his rough hands together as if in prayer. "I was at St. Mary's church in Milton. Everywhere I find a church, I light a candle and pray for those I left behind. The vicar there, Reverend Morrison, he will remember me—though I did not give him my real name. He could see I was living rough and gave me some food. He even let me warm myself in the vestry."

Milton was the village just south of Saffron Weald. It would be easy to check his alibi with the vicar.

Imogen was not ready to trust this shabby, bedraggled man, and thought she had him in a lie. "How did you know Judith had been poisoned and brought to Parkford if you were in Milton?"

"The cleaning lady at the church, she has a friend in Saffron Weald who told her how the new headmistress had been poisoned and how the job of head at that school must be cursed." His careworn expression softened. "I walked to Saffron Weald terrified that my connection to the Bolsheviks was the reason Judith had been targeted. I spent the night in a field and this morning asked a farmer where the closest hospital was. Hearing my accent, he asked if I was a refugee and if I was ill. I said yes. It wasn't entirely a lie."

"Did you know this was the second attempt on her life?" asked Ophelia.

Mikhail grabbed Judith's hand. "No!"

Imogen thought of the conversation she and her sister had on the bus on the way over. No Bolshevik spy would have a thorough grasp of the inner workings of the village amateur dramatics society, or the schedule of a country headmistress.

She opened her mouth to share this revelation when a nurse appeared at Judith's bedside.

"I'm sorry, but visiting hours are over." She gestured firmly toward the door. "Miss Rutherford needs her rest."

As they gathered their things, Judith caught Ophelia's sleeve. "Wait," she whispered, her profile suddenly tight with anxiety. "I've had some curious dreams as I've hovered between life and death and some of my life's events have flashed before my eyes. Most of it is vague and fuzzy but I have remembered something about the night of the dress rehearsal with some clarity..."

CHAPTER 24

The Admiral's Last Bow

"Incroyable!" cried Pierre, pouring himself another glass of red wine at the twins' battered kitchen table. "That filigree key is to a safe 'olding anti-Lenin documents? It sounds crazy."

"It sounds no more nutty to me than learning that both of you were spies before the war," retorted Imogen.

"Touché!" he responded, cutting himself another slice of cake. "And you say that Judith has a hazy memory of seeing a familiar scar?"

"Yes. But she cannot remember who bore the scar or what it signifies, after her close call with death." Imogen drew a frustrated hand across her forehead.

"That would certainly be reason enough for someone to kill her," Ophelia said. "Someone living quietly among us, carefully disguised, while concealing a criminal past."

"A person with something to hide, masquerading as a model citizen right under our noses," agreed Imogen. "I don't know about you, lovey, but I find this alternative vastly more satisfying than our other theories."

Ophelia stretched out her legs. "So, what are we going to do about it?"

"Well, the funeral for Nicholas Jones is tomorrow. I say we let all this percolate for the day then come up with a solid plan."

"That sounds like a very good idea," agreed Pierre. "And before all that exhausting intellectual exercise, I propose taking in a talkie at the cinema in Parkford after the funeral. There's a new picture about a pirate, if you can believe it."

"Good idea, ducky! I'm rather in the mood for some relaxing swashbuckling after all this intense drama," replied Ophelia.

The phone rang and Imogen, leaving the courting couple in the kitchen, went to answer it.

"Hello, Imogen." She recognized Matilda's voice. "We're going to resume our rehearsals the day after the funeral. Nicholas Jones' wife called me to ask if I would play the organ for the service and then assured me that moving forward with the play is what her husband would have wanted. Do you think Pierre is game?"

"Certainly. You can count us in," said Imogen. "See you tomorrow."

She rushed back to the warmth of the kitchen catching the lovebirds in a kiss. "Forget the talkie! You need to run lines, Pierre. You're going to be the admiral in the *Pirate's Fiancée*."

As is often the case at funerals, they learned things about Nicholas Jones they had not known, such as his penchant for pickled fish and his love of the seaside. The small Saffron Weald church was bursting with friends and relatives as Nicholas Jones had only reached the age of forty-nine. Among the wreaths and bouquets of flowers, someone had placed the admiral's hat in the middle of the coffin. Its presence made Imogen tear up.

After the service, in the village hall, the WI was in full swing, providing the funeral luncheon, with Mildred browbeating the other members. Thus far, though their mother had been recognized by the guild, the twins had resisted the pressure to join.

Wearing a broad rimmed, black mourning hat, Matilda claimed a seat at their table as the WI delivered sandwiches and fruit under Mildred's strict command.

"You played beautifully," commented Ophelia.

"The choir number set just the right tone," replied Matilda. She met Pierre's eye. "Have you been practicing the part?"

"We spent yesterday evening going through it," replied Ophelia.

"Honestly, I'm more worried about everyone's focus. It's one thing to say the show must go on, but after losing a cast member..." She trailed off, taking a sip of her tea.

Harriet and Harold Cleaver paused at their table. "It's a grave day so I shan't ham it up."

Harriet rolled her eyes and pushed him to another table. "Honestly, man. It's a funeral, for crying out loud."

On the other side of the hall, Imogen heard the familiar engine-splutter laugh of Reverend Cresswell which abruptly ended, as if he suddenly remembered where he was. His celery-like wife, Prudence, scanned the crowd as if worried his flock would judge him harshly for his levity at such a time.

"There aren't too many lines to learn," said Matilda to Pierre, as if no one had interrupted her. "And one main solo."

Pierre pointed a fork at her. "About that ..."

"I know you can't really sing. So just say the words in time to the music. A lot of great stage actors do that."

Relief flooded Pierre's handsome face. "That is a marvelous suggestion."

Ophelia had run through the song with him the previous evening, and though his speaking voice was quite lyrical, it soon became apparent he could not hold a tune. Matilda's suggestion was an ideal solution.

All the members of the cast had come to the funeral to pay their respects. Maggie and her husband Ed acknowledged the twins and Matilda as they passed by. Maggie's terrified countenance had improved since she had spoken to the inspector about her felonious brother-in-law. Southam had assured her they were looking into Bob Sugden's suspect 'pot of gold' and were keeping a keen eye on him.

Kitty and Celina waved from a table across the room. Kitty looked even thinner, if that were possible. They would have to re-fit the costumes if this persisted.

Des had generously donated a barrel of beer from the pub and was serving drinks. Holding a mug beneath the barrel for Reggie, whose polka dot bow tie bobbed with each movement of his Adam's apple, the pair chatted companionably. Catching Imogen's eye, Des raised the beer mug in a half-salute before turning back to his duties behind the barrel.

Alice stopped to give the twins a quick hug. "How are the sandwiches?"

"Delicious as usual," replied Matilda. "Your bread is without equal."

She blushed a little as she and Archie moved past.

The Widow Jones floated around the hall, the latest grandbaby on her hip, thanking people and sharing little anecdotes. Arriving at their table she bestowed a watery smile.

"Such a great turnout. Thank you so much for coming. And Matilda, what is a funeral without the sacred music?"

"He was a lovely man," said Ophelia blandly. She had only recently met the farmer when he began working on the musical as he was over fifteen years younger than them.

"He was. Do you know, he brought me fresh wildflowers every day in summer?" Her voice cracked and she bounced the baby to compose herself. "Don't know what I shall do without him."

This was a matter of great concern to the village since there were no sons to take over. The four people at the table all stared at their sandwiches.

"I'm going to live with my Lily and her husband. They live in West Morley and have a lovely big house."

"And the farm?" asked Pierre.

"It's up for sale. Been in our family for over three hundred years but all good things must come to an end. That's what I tell myself about Nicholas, he was too good for this world. No use harping on about it being an accident. It won't bring him back, will it?"

"It's a shame you have to move away," said Pierre. "You'll be missed."

Mrs. Jones swallowed hard. "Did you see the lovely flowers? All the farm hands pitched in and got one, and the WI, of course. Even Rex Stout sent a lovely spray. I didn't think he really knew Nicholas, but he said they passed the time of day when he was at the hall."

As she spoke, Imogen caught sight of the back of the custodian's brown coverall. He'd have to work late to get the place clean for tomorrow's rehearsal.

"Well, I'd best move on. Just wanted to thank everyone."

"I need to use the ladies' room," said Imogen, pushing out her chair as soon as Mrs. Jones had left. "Won't be a tick."

She made her way through the crowded hall, nodding and smiling as she went, and out into the little hallway that housed the toilets.

"Afternoon, Mr. Stout," she said as she brushed past him.

"Afternoon." He made a show of lifting the persistent brown cap from his head as he bid her good day.

She joined the end of the line in the crowded bathroom, behind Patricia Snodgrass.

"Imogen. Sorry to meet under such sad circumstances but it was a lovely service."

"It was." Imogen noticed the damp hankie and red blotches on Patricia's cheek.

"Did you know Farmer Jones well?"

"Not really." She sniffed. "It's just I was wondering who would have come to my funeral if *I* had accidentally drunk from the poisoned glass."

Patricia was anything but maudlin usually.

"Now, now. No need to think such depressing thoughts, lovey."

"Funerals do that to me. It's not like I'm universally loved or anything. And what have I really done with my life? I have accumulated an extensive collection of rare stamps. So what?" She gripped Imogen's arm. "I want to *do* something. Before I'm too old."

"Ophelia and I were thinking of going on a grand adventure to the Continent."

"Perfect! I have some savings put by. Let me know the dates."

Imogen's lips flapped in distress. She had not meant the comment as an invitation, but one of the stall doors opened and Patricia disappeared. *Oh dear!* Ophelia would not thank her for this.

She was still considering the misunderstanding as she washed her hands.

"Ready for tomorrow?" Pru Cresswell caught her eye in the mirror.

"I suppose so. We've been working with Pierre. I think it will be rather droll to have the British admiral played by a Frenchman."

"Napoleonic," chuckled Pru drying her hands on the towel roll.

The ladies' room door opened and Kitty entered. "I was hoping I'd catch you. Jack has left. Gone back to Liverpool. I told him the police were still interested in him for the murder, which spooked him. He took his trunk and caught the train."

"Did he say anything prior to departing?"

Kitty glanced over her shoulder before speaking, checking the room was empty. "He told me he *did* break into our house that night and sat in the living room deciding what to do. Then he thought he heard my dad and scarpered but thinks he may have dropped his cigarette in his haste. He came down to Meadowshire because the guilt was eating away at him. It won't bring my family back, but I feel better knowing it was an accident rather than someone setting the fire on purpose."

Imogen wrapped her in a hug. She was waif thin under her clothes. "I'm glad. Now you can really begin again."

As if reading Imogen's mind about the way she had mislead

everyone, she said, "The inspector came with me to see my headmistress. I explained why I had not told the whole truth on my application. She was very understanding."

Imogen knew Inspector Southam to be a very busy man and her opinion of him shot up.

"Are you ready for rehearsal tomorrow?"

Kitty blinked slowly. "I am but I'm afraid all this has made me lose my appetite. My dresses might not fit."

"Don't you worry about it. That's easily fixed."

Kitty made a half-hearted attempt at washing her hands. "What about Miss Rutherford? Will she be well enough?"

"Heaven help us all, Mildred has offered to take her place." They shared a grimace. "Though I understand Judith will be released tomorrow, she's still rather weak and we don't want to put her life at risk again."

"Did you ever discover who poisoned her?"

This was a sore point. Pierre had returned the key to Mikhail and upon a cursory look, the documents appeared to back up his claims. He had been transported to London with his papers for a scheduled interview with the thin man in Whitehall who had first shared Martov's dossier with them. The British government was extremely interested in intelligence on the inner workings of Lenin's reign, and even though he had died five years ago, they hoped Mikhail's information would help them understand more about the totalitarian government of Stalin who had replaced him. The papers also served to acquit Mikhail Martov of the attempted murder of Judith Rutherford.

They were back to square one. Almost.

"As a matter of fact, we have not. All our previous suspects, though far from innocent, have been cleared in this particular matter."

"I feel nervous about continuing with the rehearsals when the murderer is still at large." Kitty's green eyes widened. "And I'd like to go home. Judith's sister is nice and everything, but I feel like I'm a burden."

"I don't think you have anything to worry about. Judith was

definitely the target. It should be safe to go home."

Kitty did not look convinced.

Returning to their table, Imogen opened her mouth to confess her faux pas with Patricia, when Mildred sauntered over and interrupted her.

Addressing Matilda, she said, "You don't have to worry about Judith's dress not fitting me, I've almost finished sewing my own."

Ophelia bit her tongue though she sorely wanted to make a comment about Mildred's presumption in assuming she would be allowed to fill the spot.

"And I've been rehearsing the songs."

Fortunately for everyone, the chaperone had no solos.

"And I suggest we get rid of the idea of having any liquid in the glasses. We can mime drinking perfectly well."

Matilda's jaw clenched.

Imogen's lips narrowed into a tight line. *Keep to your own garden, Mildred.*

Pierre moved his chair back and Ophelia was grateful that it would bring the awkward moment to a natural conclusion. But instead of taking the hint, Mildred pulled a paper from her pocket.

"Since I'm now a key player, I took the liberty of re-blocking the promenade scene."

How like Mildred to seize upon Judith's tragedy as her opportunity to appropriate command of the entire production.

Face scarlet, Matilda mumbled something unintelligible and bolted, leaving Mildred gaping after her. "Where are her manners?"

Pierre, ever the diplomat, smoothed the moment. "I'm sure Matilda has much to organize with so little time to get ready for tomorrow."

Still holding the list of 'suggestions' as though it were a royal proclamation, Mildred huffed and turned on her heel.

As they prepared to leave, Imogen overheard Des talking to Mrs. Jones.

"The admiral's hat on the coffin was the perfect touch."

Mrs. Jones dabbed her eyes. "He was a farmer by profession, but his real calling was the stage. That hat was a symbol of his talents."

Just as they were exiting, Imogen saw Rex heading for the broom cupboard. Their day was over but his was just starting.

"Ready for tomorrow?" Ophelia asked Pierre, "or do you want to come home with us for one last practice?"

"I'd like to try pacing the spoken lyrics with the melody, if it's all the same to you?"

She slipped her arm through his and pulled Pierre close. "I'd like nothing better."

"Another dress rehearsal," said Imogen with a shiver, matching her stride to theirs. "Let's hope this one goes better than the first."

CHAPTER 25

Cues and Clues

P andemonium reigned supreme.

The whole messy dress rehearsal began to unfold like an abysmal déjà-vu – no, worse – like a horrible nightmare, because this time, Mildred the Dreaded had been given a more central role. Personalities such as hers could not resist snatching a mile when offered an inch. Mildred had stepped into poor Judith's part with the same forceful efficiency she brought to jam competitions and parish council meetings, wielding her supposed authority like a weapon. She had already reorganized the prop table, rewritten three stage directions and droned on and on, insisting that her dress was the finest example of needlecraft in the entire production.

To make things worse, the younger pirates, confined indoors by a day of relentless rain, bounced around like excited fleas pushing everyone's patience to the limit.

Matilda appeared ready to explode, her face the same shade of crimson as the velvet drapes. Bringing her fingers to her mouth, she produced an ear-splitting whistle.

"Mildred! Imogen is the stage manager. Keep to your own duties, *please*! Boys! Quiet or I will find someone else for your parts. Now, everyone go to the side you should be on." She ran a palm across her sweaty forehead as she held the open script in the other and nodded to Ophelia who began the opening overture.

Suddenly, order emerged from turmoil as Imogen pulled the curtain ropes closed while Reverend Cresswell, who had replaced Pierre, flicked switches for the overhead lights and Des Ale and Ed Sugden maneuvered the railings onto the stage for the promenade scene. From the other side, Pru's thumbs-up confirmed her actors were in place. After a quick glance checking the actors on Imogen's own side, she pulled the ropes again. The curtains swept back and the beautifully painted backdrop and the reverend's lighting cues, transformed the stage into a fashionable beach. The four leading ladies and Des entered from opposite sides.

Mildred, her gown rather too fancy for a mere chaperone, and wearing an excessive amount of badly applied greasepaint, began to walk with exaggerated steps as if she were in a pantomime. Imogen bit her lip as she watched the parasol swing wildly, almost hitting Kitty in the face. Kitty ducked and positioned herself near the railing to begin her solo as she and the pirate, Lucky Blackwood, first lay eyes on each other.

From her position in the wings, Imogen caught snippets of whispered commentary from the actors on her side of the action. "Miss Rutherford made the chaperone seem dignified," murmured Sally Pratt, "Mildred's playing it as though she's auditioning for the part of a vaudeville villain."

"Did you see how she practically shoved poor Kitty aside to get more of the spotlight?" said someone else. "Judith gracefully stepped into the background to let the younger actresses shine."

"Mildred is wielding that parasol like a weapon," chuckled Pierre.

Imogen paused, watching Mildred march as if she were leading a military parade rather than chaperoning a young lady at a coastal town.

The rest of the ladies in the promenade scene, joined in a song to warn Kitty's character against setting her cap at a person unknown to her mother. What Mildred lacked in Judith's natural talent, the other singers graciously disguised, their strong voices weaving protectively around her uncertain notes. The scene ended with Kitty surreptitiously handing Blackwood, dressed incognito as a gentleman, her card.

Imogen tugged on the curtain ropes, after grappling them from Collin, and the men ran on to replace the railing with the cutout of the pirate ship.

Surprisingly, things were flowing smoothly, everyone remembering their lines. Even the sailor's hornpipe did not leave those spectating in stitches, as it unintentionally had the last time.

Imogen met her sister's eye with concern as the scene changed for the ladies' dinner, the very moment where the tragedy was set in motion during the last rehearsal. However, blessedly, none of the glasses contained liquid and the scene continued without incident.

The set changed again, returning to the seaside, and Pierre stepped out onto the stage, dressed as the admiral. Ophelia's throat tightened as her fingers faltered on the keys, Imogen's hands clutched the black curtains of the wings, and the entire cast seemed to freeze in tableau. For one terrible heartbeat, time stopped, tangled in morbid memory, past and present merging – another admiral, another rehearsal, another moment when none of the cast knew they stood on the precipice of catastrophe. In that terrible, haunted moment, every eye fixed on Pierre, every mind walking the same dark path back to that other performance.

As Pierre began to talk-sing his solo, the entire company seemed to breathe again as the dreaded moment passed safely into memory. Even Mildred, so intent on stamping her authority on every scene, softened at the edges as the moment passed without incident.

As Molly crossed his path, Pierre stopped and bowed, introducing himself to the fiancée's mother. His perfect execution of the song with the hint of French accent, coupled with Molly's magnificent soprano, was sensational and Matilda couldn't help applauding as the pair walked off the stage arm in arm.

Imogen closed the curtains again and ran to change the backdrop as her arm muscles burned. The men rolled out the cut-out ship and Ophelia began the introduction for the next song as the reverend helped Imogen by opening the curtains.

"Ahh!" A juvenile cry split the air and the music stopped abruptly as heads poked out from the wings.

Tommy had tried jumping out from the top of the pirate ship, but caught his foot and fell, and was now sprawled on the floor, blood pouring from his nose.

"Give me strength! Rex! Rex! We need a cleanup, pronto!" Matilda spun on her heel. "I asked him to stick around. Where *is* that man?"

Tommy twisted and groaned, blood dripping all over his costume as Pru ran to his aid.

"I suppose blood on a pirate's outfit isn't the end of the world," commented the reverend. "They have a reputation for being rather *blood-thirsty,* I understand." He descended into his signature, spluttering laugh at his own joke.

The door to the kitchen swung open and Rex appeared with a mop and bucket. "Hold your horses," he mumbled. "I'm coming." He limped his way to the stage and up the side stairs as Pru prepared to usher Tommy off. But as Rex leaned over his bucket, Tommy skidded in his own blood, elbows windmilling, knocking the brown, flat cap right off Rex's head, accidentally pushing Prudence to the floor who took Des down with her. The mop and sword clattered to the floor as the custodian snatched at his cap, ramming it back onto his head before grabbing the abandoned mop and dealing with the mess. Des's legs wiggled in the air like an overturned tortoise.

Imogen looked up to find Ophelia giving her the death stare.

Having been released from the hospital, Judith was back at her tiny cottage next to the school. Nodding to the police officer stationed outside her door and armed with a bouquet of flowers, the twins appeared on her doorstep where Judith's sister, Emily, received them enthusiastically. "So many visitors. What a lovely place this is. Come on in." She took the flowers. "My sister is in the parlor. I'll just put these in a vase." She pushed open the door to the sitting room for them before heading to the kitchen.

Judith sat in a wing back chair flanked by Mikhail on one side and Kitty on the other. The morning light through the lace curtains cast strange shadows across her chalky, drawn face.

"Ophelia! Imogen! How lovely. Have a seat." She lifted a hand in welcome but it dropped to her lap, her voice hardly louder than a ghost's whisper. The twins noticed how Mikhail's hand tightened protectively on the arm of Judith's chair.

"How are you feeling?" asked Ophelia.

"A bit like I've fought a battle and lost, to be honest," she wheezed.

"I don't doubt it," said Imogen. She glanced at Kitty. "Would you mind getting me a drink, my dear?"

A question appeared on Judith's brow as the tiny teacher left the room. Her eyes, still sharp despite her weakness, darted between the twins.

"We need to ask you something."

CHAPTER 26

Final Reckoning

In the comfort and security of Judith's cozy cottage, with the fire crackling and spreading its cheery warmth, the twins discussed their latest discovery. Even before they could finish explaining their current theory, recognition bloomed over Judith's fragile features.

"The scar," she murmured, trembling fingers finding their way to her own forehead. "That's what I saw in my dream. I haven't thought of it for over fourteen years."

The clock on the mantelpiece ticked steadily as Judith recounted the sad saga from the Great War, her voice growing stronger with each miserable sentence, helping Imogen and Ophelia to finally unravel the mystery that linked long-buried history to current events. At the sisters' suggestion, Judith invited Inspector Southam to tea at her cottage.

His arrival left damp impressions of his boots on the doormat as Ophelia ushered him in.

"Well, well, well. You two have done it again." After listening to Judith's story, the inspector tipped his hat with his pencil in a trademark move, the corner of his mouth twitching with something approaching admiration.

"As I see it, we can do this now and interrupt your play again or we can do the big reveal as a part of the finale." Scratching his head with the pencil he continued, "It's all the same to me. We'll keep the police officer outside your house, so you'll be safe, Miss Rutherford."

"And I am sleeping on the sofa to protect her, also," said Mikhail, his accent thickening with determination as he squeezed Judith's hand.

Southam's bottom lip disappeared into his mustache, his eyes darting between the four faces in the room. "What do you think? There are things I need to check anyway, make sure we have this all buttoned up, but it's your decision, Miss Rutherford." He leaned back, the chair creaking underneath his weight. "Don't think they'll get suspicious if we wait. No one here is going to raise the alarm. And it would be nice to have everything shipshape—" he caught himself, lips quirking. "Oh, excuse the pun."

Judith straightened in her chair, the first suggestion that her former strength was returning. "I want to see the play, and everyone's worked so hard that I don't want it to be cancelled again. Let's make a splash and reveal the murderer at the end, as you suggest, Inspector. They killed an innocent bystander with their reckless behavior *and* made an attempt on my own life. I don't believe they merit our discretion. In fact, they deserve to be outed in dramatic fashion." Her words dropped to a whisper that held the steel of an army nurse and headmistress beneath its softness. "It will be a great revenge."

Heat radiated from the packed bodies in the village hall, condensation beginning to form on the tall windows. The final act loomed, and miraculously, no disasters had struck. Imogen parted the heavy curtains just enough to see Matilda beaming in the front row, flanked by Judith and Mikhail, and to survey the back of the overflowing hall. Her gaze swept over the enthusiastic crowd, their faces still bright with laughter from the last scene, before settling on Ophelia seated at the piano. Her sister's fingers danced through the interlude, buying precious seconds for the scene change. Against all odds, the farce had landed perfectly – every joke, every mishap, every confused identity had delighted the audience exactly as intended, especially Reggie's variation. Imogen took a deep breath, inhaling the mingled scents of stage-makeup, dust, and excitement.

Walking back to the sidelines, she nodded to Des, his chest puffed out in the dapper morning suit, and pulled the curtain ropes to reveal the wedding scene. The reverend stood center stage, open prayer book in his hand, Des positioned to his left. Through the wings, Imogen caught sight of Kitty adjusting her long-sleeved wedding gown, the intricate beadwork created by Harriet sparkling under the lights.

Ophelia's nimble fingers crashed down on the keys, thundering out the wedding march. Kitty's cue. The crowd gasped as she glided onto the stage, the majestic train trailing behind her like seafoam.

The reverend's familiar tones boomed through the hall. "If anyone knows of any reason why this couple should not be joined in holy matrimony..."

One by one, the guests popped up like weeds in a garden, each objection more outlandish than the last. The audience burst into peals of laughter while Molly, clutching her pearls, feigned horror that her daughter had almost married a pirate king.

Pierre threw himself into his role as the admiral, his eyebrows working overtime as he declared, "I suspected I'd encountered this Lucky Blackwood before – in decidedly less favorable circumstances!" His voice dropped to a stage whisper that nonetheless carried to the back row: "And I believe he was standing on the edge of a plank at the time."

The audience roared as the pirates swarmed the stage in a coordinated chaos of stomping boots and swinging swords. Kitty's shriek could have shattered glass as she threw herself into Lucky's arms, who hoisted her over his shoulder and ran offstage, brandishing his own sword at the wedding guests.

The curtains closed to raucous cheers and the ensemble gathered behind them for the curtain call, adjusting costumes, wiping sweat, and exchanging triumphant glances.

Backstage, a darker gathering took shape as several uniformed officers slipped into position, unnoticed.

Reverend Cresswell wrestled with the ropes for the encore and the curtain fabric swayed with the grace of a drunken bridesmaid. The ensemble bowed as one, and the whole room rose to their feet, the wooden floorboards vibrating with stomping appreciation. Molly, Kitty, Celina and Mildred stepped forward, hands clasped, beside Des and Pierre as the crowd went wild. Des gestured to Matilda who stood at her seat, facing the crowd to roars and cheers.

Des beckoned for her to join them on stage. Her reluctance melted as the audience's enthusiasm washed over her. Cheeks burning crimson, she complied, kissing and hugging everyone in the cast, leaving lipstick marks on cheeks and tears on shoulders.

When the energy of the audience waned, Matilda pushed her hands down for everyone to quieten.

"Thank you so much for coming to honor Nicholas Jones." Her throat caught on the name. "All the money from today's ticket sales will be donated to the Jones family." The applause erupted again drowning her out. She waited, hands clasped at her heart, until it died down.

"I also want to thank everyone who has helped in any way with tonight's production, the scene designer, the set creators, the costume crew. Who am I forgetting?" She glanced at Imogen. "Oh, yes. And special thanks to our custodian, Mr. Rex Stout. Rex? Rex? Come on up here."

Every head in the room swiveled, trying to discover the whereabouts of the reclusive caretaker.

In the shadows by the exit, someone gave Rex a firm push between the shoulder blades. Matilda caught sight of the movement. "There he is. Come on up here, Rex."

A confused ripple of applause sounded through the hall as Mr.

Stout, head down, stumbled down the aisle and onto the stage, the floorboards creaking under his uneven gait.

Inspector Southam pushed his bulk through the ensemble, positioning himself beside Rex, who still had not raised his eyes from the floor.

"Hello, Mr. Stout." Southam's deep voice cut through the noise like a knife.

Beneath the blistering spotlights, Rex froze. The silence in the hall grew thick enough to touch. The custodian had nowhere to run. He was well and truly trapped.

Resembling a marionette with severed strings, Rex's whole frame slumped. Southam reached over to remove the custodian's flat cap with deliberate slowness.

The stage lights caught the jagged scar that ran along his receding hairline, illuminating it in harsh relief against his pale skin. It's curves and hooks resembled a broken treble clef lying on its side.

The audience hushed in bewilderment.

"This theater production suffered a terrible tragedy," began Southam, his speech filling every corner of the silent hall. "An innocent man accidentally drank poison meant for another of the actors."

A wave of whispers surged through the crowd. In the front row, Judith's hand found Mikhail's, her knuckles white.

"It must have been a terrible shock when the wrong person died." He circled Rex slowly, the cap still dangling from his fingers. "But the problem still needed to be solved, and in the sanctuary of the schoolhouse full of unsuspecting children, the killer struck again."

Rex's shoulders hunched further, his gaze fixed on a knot in the wooden stage floor.

"He failed a second time." Southam's cadence hardened. "A terrible murderer but a lucky wretch; he managed to strike twice without any witnesses." He pushed against the caretaker's shoulder with one finger. "Because who notices a custodian? He can appear in any number of places without raising eyebrows."

Southam turned to face the audience. "And the problem that stumped law enforcement was motive. Without it, we had no idea why Miss Rutherford was being targeted."

At the mention of her name, heads turned toward Judith in the front row, her face now set in grim satisfaction.

"Then by chance, your own Tommy Fletcher accidentally knocked off Mr. Stout's hat during rehearsal and your local sleuths' minds went into overdrive. Was the singular scar that was always hidden under the hat, the key to the whole case? The 'Detective Duo' immediately asked Miss Rutherford if she had ever nursed a wounded soldier with such a distinctive scar during the war."

Rex's hands clenched into fists at his sides.

"Their question unlocked a buried memory that had begun to emerge through her state of unconsciousness. Miss Rutherford told them of a soldier who had been hit in the head by shrapnel."

Watching Judith as the inspector spoke, Imogen witnessed memories flickering across her features.

"It was not a deep wound, but it was distinctive. Unfortunately for him, the soldier was to be sent back to the front as soon as the superficial cut healed. However, he returned less than a week later with a gunshot wound to the foot." Southam's eyebrows rose significantly. "Judith Rutherford was certain the injury was self-inflicted, but the hospital was snowed under with casualties, and the doctors too overworked to listen. The ignoble soldier was sent home with others who were to be invalided out of the army."

As the inspector paused, Rex's labored breathing became audible in the deathly silence of the hall.

"Life went on and thousands more soldiers came through Miss Rutherford's ward. The disgraced soldier was forgotten on the ash pile of war." Southam paced the stage, Rex Stout shrinking from his movements. "The world conflict finally ended and Miss Rutherford returned home to Somerset to teach. Mr. Stout moved away from his home in Sussex, grew his hair, adopted a beard and mustache and started wearing a cap to hide the distinguishing scar. He settled in Saffron Weald, hidden and invisible as the church custodian." Inspector Southam cleared his throat. "Then Mr. Stout's luck began to change. The position for a replacement headmistress in Saffron Weald opened up and Miss Rutherford applied." His words took on a contemplative tone. "I imagine Mr. Stout recognized Miss Rutherford right away but hoped the change in his appearance and his position as a lowly caretaker were protection enough. Time went on and the former nurse showed no signs of recognizing him. He was safe." He took a breath, stalling to let the word 'safe' sink in.

"Safe, that is, until a primary school assembly to recognize those who had served honorably in the war." Southam's pitch rose again. "Each veteran soldier was presented with a special remembrance wreath and childish medals made by the children. As a little tyke placed the ribbon over Mr. Stout's head, the cap was knocked askew."

Rex's head finally snapped up, his eyes meeting the inspector's with a mixture of fear and resignation.

"I bet you were petrified. Panicked. Had the headmistress seen the scar? You couldn't take the risk." Southam handed the cap to a uniformed officer who had appeared at his side. "You tried to keep out of sight as much as possible and began to plan how best to eliminate the problem."

At last, Rex spoke, his voice rough with emotion. "She would have reported me to the war office." The words fell, shattering the silence as decisively as rocks hitting calm water. "I would have lost my pension. My standing." His defense trailed off. "Everything I'd built here would have been destroyed."

The uniformed officers moved in, one on each side of the caretaker. For a fleeting moment he struggled. "I'm right sorry about the farmer."

As the policemen led Rex away, his limping gait – once assumed to be from age or labor – now revealed itself as the final piece of evidence: the self-inflicted wound that had saved him from the front lines but ultimately led him back to Judith Rutherford.

CHAPTER 27

A Satisfying Encore

D es threw an after-party for the entire cast at the Dog and Whistle. Mildred imbibed one too many snowballs and had to be transported home by Reggie, while singing, 'If I Were The Only Girl in the World' at the top of her lungs. Tommy and Collin had gone around sipping the empties and thrown up all over Des's Persian rug. Even Judith had managed to make an appearance for a few minutes.

"She's looking better already," Matilda had whispered to Imogen, watching the mysterious Russian who hovered at her elbow with interest.

"Nothing like seeing justice served to aid in a speedy recovery," chuckled Imogen.

Pru and the reverend walked by and she caught a fragment of their conversation. "To think our caretaker was a coward and a murderer!"

Matilda rolled her eyes. "Hidden in plain sight. It doesn't bear thinking about."

Mikhail helped Judith walk over to the twins' table. "The real irony is that I didn't even notice his scar the day of the assembly."

The twins exchanged a tortured glance, the weight of needless tragedy settling between them. Two lives forever altered, one ended, all because of a fear that existed only in Rex's mind.

"It was Rex's guilty conscience that condemned him, prompting him to attack," said Ophelia. "What a waste."

They watched as the Russian escorted Judith out to her car.

Tapping her chin, Matilda asked, "She knew Mikhail twenty years ago, correct? I've been racking my brain to see if I can think of anyone from my youth who might come back and sweep me off my feet."

"Any luck?" asked Imogen, raising her glass.

"Not yet!" Matilda took another swig of her wine. "But a girl can hope."

"Judith will make a speedy recovery, I don't doubt, with a besotted Russian ensuring she follows doctor's orders," mused Imogen with a knowing smile.

Inspector Southam had made a brief appearance too, accepting a congratulatory whisky from Des before pulling the twins aside.

"Well, the Detective Duo strikes again," he said, raising his glass in a small toast. "Four out of four. Not a bad record. The Parkford station's buzzing about your talents."

"Stop it, Inspector! You're making us blush," said Imogen with a satisfied grin.

"Rex has confessed to everything," the inspector continued, lowering his voice. "He'll go straight to sentencing."

"Where did he get the poison?" Imogen asked, always practical.

"He bought it last year as rat poison for a problem in the church basement." Southam sighed heavily. "Simple as that."

"He slipped into Judith's office after fixing the plumbing issue, is my guess," said Ophelia.

"Right again. He wasn't a stranger, so no one thought twice about him being there."

The party continued around them, the cast celebrating their triumph. Molly and Celina debated which production should be their next endeavor.

"How about, *Lady Belvedere Has a Change of Heart*?" Celina insisted, waving an olive-laden toothpick for emphasis.

"Too soon for another comedy," Molly had countered. "How about a mystery?"

Everyone groaned.

"I do hope that means you'll be staying," said Ophelia.

"Oh, yes." She nodded in the inspector's direction. "We've been told that the authorities have found Bob's stash of cash and are returning it to the bank from which it was stolen. He also has to pay back what 'e spent." She cackled. "That should take 'im a while!"

"And you're not worried about him bothering your family?"

She gestured toward the inspector. "Thanks to Inspector Southam, if Bob Sugden so much as comes within ten miles of us, he'll be sent back to prison for profiting from a crime. If he stays away, the Crown will forgive that offense."

Imogen clapped her hands together. "That is good news."

As the twins prepared to leave, Imogen nudged Ophelia and tipped her head. Peter and Malcolm Cleaver were making a cozy foursome in a snug corner with Kitty and Celina.

The twins and Pierre were enjoying a late-night cup of hot cocoa beside the fire with Tiger. The old cottage creaked comfortably around them, the crackling flames and panting of the dog, the only sounds beyond their quiet conversation.

With no warning, Pierre slipped off the sofa, onto one knee in front of Ophelia and opened a black ring box.

Her hands flew to her cheeks. "Ahh! You found it!"

Pierre slid the stolen ring onto Ophelia's finger. "Ophelia Harrington. Will you marry me?"

Imogen squealed with delight.

"Of course!" Ophelia flung her arms around Pierre's neck which Tiger took as an invitation to join in.

"Silly dog!" cried Imogen, pulling on his collar.

"Where did you find it?" asked Ophelia admiring the antique ring in the firelight.

"Remember I told you that meeting 'Umble 'Enry 'ad given me an idea? I made the rounds of all the pawnshops in Meadowshire and found it lurking at a place called *Vintage Treasures* owned by a slow fellow with long, brown 'air and tired eyes that drooped."

"Was he smoking a pipe?" giggled Ophelia.

"As a matter of fact, 'e was."

"Voice like a rusty gate?" Imogen remembered the sloth well.

"I see you 'ave met the fellow."

"Indeed, we have." Ophelia could not stop admiring the ring. "He's the fellow we tangled with in the middle of the night with Tiger and the inspector on our second case. I'm surprised he's not still in jail."

Pierre made a Gallic shrug. "I know nothing about that but 'e's the one who 'ad the ring. 'E wanted to charge me £50 for something that 'ad been stolen from me. Outrageous! I got all 'ot under the jumper—"

"Collar," corrected Ophelia.

"Yes, collar. I accused 'im of stealing the ring from my shop and threatened to call the police. 'E quickly changed his note—"

"Tune."

"Ah, yes, tune, and 'anded it over saying that 'e should have known it was stolen when the chap only wanted £10. That's why it was 'idden among a lot of other rings."

Ophelia ran a finger down Pierre's nose. "You clever thing."

"When do you want to get married?"

"When do you suggest?"

"I was thinking tomorrow at two. I've already 'ad a word with Bartholomew Cresswell."

Ophelia jumped back. "You're not serious?"

"About wanting to marry you as soon as possible? I couldn't be more serious, chérie. But I understand that you might want to get a special dress and throw a small party."

"And we need to invite my niece and nephew and friends from my orchestra days and—"

He put his fingers to her lips. "I know. I cannot 'ave my own way in this. And I would like my sister to come anyway, and she will 'ave to make plans. 'Ow about June?"

"Three months?" She met her sister's eye. "Do you think we can pull it off?"

Imogen pursed her lips. "Undoubtedly, but there is something I forgot to tell you."

Both sets of eyes were on her.

"I may have accidentally told Patricia we were going on a grand tour of Europe in the spring and invited her."

"What?"

"She was getting all weepy about not having accomplished anything in her life and I tried to console her by giving her an example, but she jumped to the wrong conclusion and thought I was inviting her."

"It's true that I said I'd take you on that trip you never got to make with Wilf. But it certainly did not include Patricia Snodgrass."

"That's the thing. Patricia told Matilda, who told Harriet, who told Alice, who told Prudence who told Mildred." Imogen felt sheepish. "They've been planning it and want to go at the end of April."

"Are you seriously considering it?" asked Ophelia hardly able to believe her ears.

"The timing would be rather tight," Imogen admitted. "But you could think of it as a pre-wedding adventure."

"She has lost her mind." She looked to Pierre for confirmation.

He gestured with both hands. "You *did* promise your sister, and I will survive without you for a short time."

The fire popped and settled, sending a shower of sparks up the chimney.

"I completely understand if you want to stay here and get ready for the wedding, lovey."

"But you'll need an experienced guide. Especially since none of you have ever been before."

"I'm sure we can hire an experienced one."

Ophelia held up her hands. "Nonsense. They will just take your money and tell you rubbish." She twisted to face Pierre.

He made a bridge with his hands. "It has to be you, chérie. No one else will do."

"Fine! You've convinced me. A European tour it is. But," she wagged a finger at her sister, "we have to be back in plenty of time to finalize the wedding plans."

"Of course," Imogen beamed. "I wouldn't dream of jeopardizing your special day."

"*Our* special day," Ophelia corrected, leaning against Pierre. "You're my maid of honor, after all."

Imogen felt a sudden pang of emotion at her sister's words.

As if sensing her thoughts, Ophelia reached across to squeeze her hand. "Who says life is over by sixty?"

Tiger, sensing the emotional moment, hopped onto the sofa and wedged himself between Pierre and Ophelia, his tail thumping against the cushions.

Pierre pushed the dog away and raised his hands in the air. "*The Detective Duo Takes Paris.*"

"Very funny." Ophelia swatted his arm playfully. "Surely we can manage our Continental tour without stumbling over a corpse."

Imogen smiled. "Never say never…"

The End

BOOKS BY THIS AUTHOR

Murder At Farrington Hall

The Honorable Lady Dorothea Dorchester - Dodo to her friends - has a nose for crime and fashion. Unlucky in love but adept at sleuthing, she navigates the world of high society with intelligence and panache. When she and her sister, Lady Diantha, are invited to a party at Farrington Hall they eagerly accept. The weekend begins with a lot of promise until disaster strikes. A theft leads to murder and Dodo is called upon by her hosts to help the police, who are less than happy to have an amateur interfering. Can she win them over and solve the crime?

Murder Is Fashionable

Stylish Dodo Dorchester is a well-known patron of fashion. Hired by the famous Renee Dubois to support her line of French designs, she travels between Paris and London frequently. Arriving for the showing of the Spring 1923 collection, Dodo is thrust into her role as an amateur detective when one of the fashion models is murdered. Working under the radar of the French DCJP Inspector Roget, she follows clues to solve the crime. Will the murderer prove to be the man she has fallen for?

Murder At The Races

It is royal race day at Ascot, 1923. Lady Dorothea Dorchester,

Dodo, has been invited by her childhood friend, Charlie, to an exclusive party in a private box with the added incentive of meeting the King and Queen.Charlie appears to be interested in something more than friendship when a murder interferes with his plans. The victim is one of the guests from the box and Dodo cannot resist poking around. When Chief Inspector Blood of Scotland Yard is assigned to the case, sparks fly between them again. The chief inspector and Dodo have worked together on a case before and he welcomes her assistance with the prickly upper-class suspects. But where does this leave poor Charlie? Dodo eagerly works on solving the murder which may have its roots in the distant past. Can she find the killer before they strike again?

Murder On The Moors

When you just want to run away and nurse your broken heart but murder comes knocking. Lady Dorothea Dorchester, Dodo, flees to her cousins' estate in Dartmoor in search of peace and relaxation after her devastating break-up with Charlie and the awkward attraction to Chief Inspector Blood that caused it. Horrified to learn that the arch-nemesis from her schooldays, Veronica Shufflebottom, has been invited, Dodo prepares for disappointment. However, all that pales when one of the guests disappears after a ramble on the foggy moors. Presumed dead, Dodo attempts to contact the local police to report the disappearance only to find that someone has tampered with the ancient phone. The infamous moor fog is too thick for safe travel and the guests are therefore stranded. Can Dodo solve the case without the help of the police before the fog lifts?

Murder In Limehouse

Aristocratic star she may be, but when her new love's sister is implicated in a murder, Dodo Dorchester rolls up her designer sleeves and plunges into the slums of London.

Dodo is back from the moors of Devon and diving into fashion business for the House of Dubois with one of the most celebrated department stores in England, while she waits for a call from Rupert Danforth, her newest love interest.

Curiously, the buyer she met with at the store, is murdered that night in the slums of Limehouse. It is only of passing interest because Dodo has no real connection to the crime. Besides, pursuing the promising relationship that began in Devon is a much higher priority.

However, fate has a different plan. Rupert's sister, Beatrice, is arrested for the murder of the very woman Dodo conducted business with at the fashionable store. Now she must solve the crime to protect the man she is fast falling in love with.

Can she do it before Beatrice is sent to trial?

Murder On Christmas Eve

Dodo is invited to meet Rupert's family for Christmas. What could possibly go wrong?

Fresh off the trauma of her last case, Dodo is relieved when Rupert suggests spending Christmas with his family at Knightsbrooke Priory.

The week begins with such promise until Rupert's grandmother, Adelaide, dies in the middle of their Christmas Eve dinner. She is ninety-five years old and the whole family considers it an untimely natural death, but something seems off to Dodo who uses the moment of shock to take a quick inventory of the body. Certain clues bring her to draw the conclusion that Adelaide has been murdered, but this news is not taken well.

With multiple family skeletons set rattling in the closets, the festive week of celebrations goes rapidly downhill and Dodo fears that Rupert's family will not forgive her meddling. Can she solve the case and win back their approval?

Murder On The Med

An idyllic Greek holiday. A murdered ex-pat. Connect the victim to your tourist party, and you have a problem that only Dodo can solve.

Dodo's beau, Rupert, is to meet the Dorchesters for the first time on their annual Greek holiday. He arrives in Athens by train and her family accept him immediately. But rather than be able to enjoy private family time, an eclectic group of English tourists attach themselves to the Dorchesters, and insist on touring the Parthenon with them.

Later that night, a body is found in the very area they had visited and when Dodo realizes that it is the woman she saw earlier, near the hotel, staring at someone in their group, she cannot help but get involved. The over-worked and under-staffed local detective is more than happy for her assistance and between them they unveil all the tourists' dirty secrets.

With help from Rupert and Dodo, can the detective discover the murderer and earn himself a promotion?

Murder Spoils The Fair

A high profile national fair, a murdered model. Can Dodo solve the crime before it closes the fair?

The historic British Empire Fair of 1924 is set to be officially opened by the king at the new Wembley Stadium and Lady Dorothea Dorchester, Dodo, has an invitation.

The whole fair is an attempt to build morale after a devastating World War and the planning and preparation have been in the works for years. So much is riding on its success.

The biggest soap maker in England has been offered the opportunity to host a beauty exhibit and after a nationwide search for the ten most beautiful girls in Britain, they build an extravagant 'palace' that will feature live models representing famous women of history, including one who will represent today's modern woman. Dodo has succeeded in winning the bid to clothe Miss 1924 with fashions from the House of Dubois for whom she is a fashion ambassador.

But the fair has hardly begun when disaster strikes. One of the models is murdered. Can Dodo find the murderer before the bad PR closes the fair?

Murder Takes A Swing

High stakes, dark secrets, murder and mayhem. Can Dodo find the killer of Rupert's polo teammate without endangering their love in the process?

In Murder Takes A Swing, Dodo Dorchester finds herself drawn deep into the glamorous world of polo when one of her beaus' teammates is found murdered the night after their victorious first game of the season.

With the sport of kings as its backdrop, this gripping and unputdownable page-turner will keep you on the edge of your seat as Rupert's friends and teammates become the prime suspects in this deadly game of hidden secrets.

Dodo must use her wits to untangle a web of deceit and betrayal that threatens to unravel everything Rupert thought he knew about his friends. Will she be able to solve the case before the killer strikes again? Can their developing relationship endure the strain?

Full of charm, and suspense, this delightful 1920s cozy mystery will transport you back in time to a world of adventure, and danger, keeping you on the edge of your seat until the very last twist.

Perfect for fans of classic murder mystery novels and historical whodunnits, this is a book you won't want to miss. So, grab your mallet and join the game – the stakes are high and the secrets are deadly.

Murder Goes Jazz

The hottest American jazz band, fresh from New Orleans. A clandestine party full of 'bright young things' in the middle of London's East End. When murder kills the celebration, will Dodo catch the culprit before Scotland Yard? Or will she be the next victim?

When a legendary New Orleans jazz band arrives on Britain's balmy shores to play at a clandestine jazz party in a deserted warehouse, Dodo is more than excited. But the jubilant atmosphere takes a dark turn when a shocking murder occurs right under her nose.

With her keen mind and charming demeanor, Dodo dives into the case, navigating through a labyrinth of clues, motives, and potential suspects. As the tide of suspicion ebbs and flows, Dodo must navigate the fascinating and cut-throat world of jazz before the killer strikes a haunting final chord.

Close the blinds, grab your favorite drink, and curl up with this fun, suspenseful Golden Age cozy mystery today!

Murder In New Orleans

Solving a murder in the Big Easy is anything but.

After an invitation to visit New Orleans from Miss Lucille Bassett, famous jazz singer, Dodo and company board a luxury ocean liner and head across the pond. The climate, the food and the culture couldn't be more different from England and Dodo considers the whole trip a grand adventure.

Enjoying her role as tourist, Dodo delights in a trip on a steamer down the Mississippi, a visit to an ancient smuggler's dwelling and the hustle and bustle of Bourbon Street. At the top of her wish list, however, is dancing at Miss Bassett's famous jazz club.

On their second day in Louisiana, a terrible murder occurs without any obvious motive. Lucille implores Dodo to take the case as gangsters abound in the Prohibition Era South and have the police department in their pockets.

Dodo agrees but her sleuthing places a loved one in danger and she is torn between solving the crime for her friend or protecting those she loves.

Curl up with this delightful, pager-turner of a whodunnit that will have you on the edge of your seat until the last chapter.

Murder Midst The Diamonds

Diamonds are a girl's best friend. Murder isn't.

Love is in the air as Dodo Dorchester and Rupert Danforth prepare to announce their engagement. After a successful appointment with London's premier jeweler, plans begin for the engagement party until murder strikes at the heart of their happiness and their dream ring becomes evidence in a deadly puzzle. Dodo's dreams of a Times announcement and a fairy-tale celebration crumble faster than a dropped scone at high tea.

In a world where old money meets new, could the culprit be among London's glittering social elite or is a notorious gang of international jewel thieves behind the bloodshed?

Now, instead of planning the engagement bash, Dodo is planning interviews with suspects—and there are plenty to choose from, as she is faced with untangling a web of deception that stretches from London's criminal underground to the glamorous world of the West End.

Will she and Rupert ever be able to make their engagement official? Will Chief Inspector Blood put a spanner in the works? Will the murderer strike again before Dodo can figure it all out?

This thrilling new installment, of a beloved, charming and delightfully clever historical mystery series, is perfect for readers who adore a side of romance with their murder and a splash of scandal in their tea.

For fans of Rhys Bowen, Miss Fisher's Murder Mysteries and lovers of the Roaring Twenties, aristocratic amateur sleuths and romance-tinged mysteries.

Villlage Fetes Can Be Murder

An old mystery, a murdered stranger and a notebook full of secrets turn a quaint village upside down with fear and suspicion.

At the reading of their mother's will, the lives of twin sisters Imogen and Ophelia are changed forever. In addition to leaving them the family home in the quaint village of Saffron Weald, their mother's last request is that they retire together in the cottage, Badger's Hollow. Ophelia, a retired musician, and Imogen, a recently widowed mother of two grown children, jump at the chance since they are still in good health.

Their arrival coincides with the annual village fete, and they readily agree to lend a hand with the tug of war. However, when they go to the supply tent to retrieve the rope, they discover the body of a visiting young journalist. Before the arrival of the hapless village constable, the sisters scour the murder scene and discover several clues including a notebook in the girl's bag filled with detailed notes on the villagers including one that hits shockingly close to home. Intrigued, the discovery propels them into investigating the murder themselves, taking them on a journey fraught with suspicion, startling revelations, and danger.

Will the sisters succeed in bringing the ruthless murderer to justice or will they become victims of a predator desperate to keep their dark secrets hidden?

Join these delightful and amusing elderly sleuths on their first detecting adventure and meet a whole cast of colorful and quirky characters.

Fans of Agatha Christie's Miss Marple will fall in love with the smart and sassy sisters in this delightful new series.

Church Choirs Can Be Murder

Murder in the church choir always strikes the wrong note

Someone is stealing priceless, sacred artifacts from the church vault of the quaint English village of Saffron Weald. Ophelia, and her identical twin Imogen, are called upon to lend their sleuthing skills to discover the identity of the thief before the matter needs to be reported to church authorities, thus avoiding a scandal. But the investigation takes a sinister turn when a shocking murder occurs, thrusting the inquisitive sisters into a web of mystery and intrigue.

As they delve into the church's storied past, the suspect pool narrows to members of the church choir, and the twins face a perplexing puzzle: could the theft and murder be intertwined?

As Imogen and Ophelia follow a trail of cryptic clues with the help of their faithful dog, Tiger, they uncover secrets long buried, both within the sacred walls of the church and the confines of the ancient village. Yet, their investigation is hampered by the mysterious disappearance of a vital ledger, meticulously kept by the victim, detailing the church's priceless medieval treasures. With time running out, the resourceful twins must unravel the truth before the murderer strikes again. Rich in 1920s historical charm and laden with suspense, the second installment of this best-selling series will keep readers on the edge of their seats. Join the delightful, retired twin sisters as they embark on this quest to uncover the dark secrets lurking behind the church choir's harmonious façade.

Will they solve the murder and recover the lost treasures or will the mysteries of the past remain forever hidden.

Book Clubs Can Be Murder

Will murder pen the final chapter of the newly minted village book club?

As winter's chill descends on the picturesque village of Saffron Weald, twin sisters Imogen and Ophelia find warmth among friends in the newly formed book club. However, the cozy literary evenings take a dark turn when a historic storm batters the countryside, leaving destruction in its wake – and the tragic death of one of their club members, which the hasty police blame on nature's fury. But the sisters' instincts tell them there's much more to the story.

Armed with their innate knack for deduction, the help of their faithful dog Tiger, and the odd ride from their gorgeous French friend, Pierre, they embark on a perilous investigation. As the pair dig deeper into the victim's past, they uncover a web of secrets, deception and betrayal stretching back to wartime London.

In a village where everyone seems to have something to hide, can Imogen and Ophelia separate fact from fiction before the final page turns on their own story?

Book Clubs Can Be Murder is a cozy mystery that proves even the most genteel of settings can harbor deadly secrets. Perfect for fans of Agatha Christie and Jessica Fletcher, this twisty tale of sisterly sleuthing will keep you guessing until the very end.

Death At A Christmas Party

A merry Christmas party with old friends. A dead body in the kitchen. A reluctant heroine. Sounds like a recipe for a jolly festive murder mystery!

It is 1928 and a group of old friends gather for their annual Christmas party. The food, drink and goodwill flow, and everyone has a rollicking good time.

When the call of nature forces the accident-prone Percy Pontefract up, in the middle of the night, she realizes she is in need of a little midnight snack and wanders into the kitchen. But she gets more than she bargained for when she trips over a dead body.

Ordered to remain in the house by the grumpy inspector sent to investigate the case, Percy stumbles upon facts about her friends that shake her to the core and cause her to suspect more than one of them of the dastardly deed.

Finally permitted to go home, Percy tells her trusty cook all the awful details. Rather than sympathize, the cook encourages her to do some investigating of her own. After all, who knows these people better than Percy? Reluctant at first, Percy begins poking into her friends' lives, discovering they all harbor dark secrets. However, none seem connected to the murder…at first glance.

Will Percy put herself and her children in danger before she can solve the case that has the police stumped?

Death Is A Blank Canvas

An invitation-only art exhibition. A rising star cut down in his prime. The only suspects, family and a handful of aristocrats. How will Percy navigate these treacherous waters to solve the callous crime?

In this gripping sequel, Percy Pontefract finds herself entangled in a twisted web of murder and lies that strikes painfully close to home, when her talented cousin is brutally killed as the curtain rises on his inaugural modern art exhibition in the heart of London.

The shadow of suspicion looms over everyone present; Percy's colorful relatives and a number of enigmatic aristocrats. When circumstances thrust Percy into detection, she is soon caught up in a dangerous game of cat and mouse as she unravels the truth and concludes that the solution to the murder lies beneath layers of paint, privilege and pretension. She must rely on intuition and luck to avoid becoming the next victim.

Set against a backdrop of the glamorous world of fine art and filled with a cast of eccentric characters, Death Is a Blank Canvas, is a rollicking good whodunnit that will keep you guessing until the very end.

FREE AI AUDIO

Thanks for reading my book. As a special gift I am offering free ai audio of some of my books using my own voice.

payhip.com/AnnSutton

AFTERWORD

I was born and bred in England but I live in the USA. I was advised by my editor to use American spelling as this is by far my largest audience. Since it's just me, I don't have time to create a separate version with British spelling.

ABOUT THE AUTHOR

Ann Sutton

Agatha Christie plunged Ann Sutton into the fabulous world of reading when she was 10. She was never the same. She read every one of Christie's books she could lay her hands on. Mysteries remain her favorite genre to this day - so it was only natural that she would eventually write my own.

Born and raised in England, Ann graduated college with a double honors in Education and French. During her year abroad teaching English in France, she met her Californian husband. Married in London, they moved to California after her graduation.

Together with their growing family they bounced all around the United States, finally settling in the foothills of the Rocky Mountains.

After dabbling with writing over the years, Ann finally began in earnest when her youngest was in middle school. Covid lockdown pushed her to take her writing even more seriously and so was born the best-selling Dodo Dorchester Mystery Series. To date over 230,000 units have been sold or read on KU. You can find out more about Ann Sutton at annsuttonsuthor.com.

ACKNOWLEDGEMENT

A lot of people have helped me on my writing journey but no one more than my husband.

Printed in Great Britain
by Amazon

63038844R10137